A CELTIC LITURGY

For Tony and Barbara

A CELTIC LITURGY

Pat Robson

Originally published in Great Britain in 2000
by HarperCollinsReligious

Published in Great Britain in 2008
in hardback

Society for Promoting Christian Knowledge
36 Causton Street
London SW1P 4ST
www.spck.org.uk

Reprinted once
Second (paperback) edition 2015

British Library Cataloguing-in-Publication Data
A catalogue record for this book is available from the
British Library

ISBN 978–0–281–07410–5

Printed and bound in Great Britain by Clays Ltd, Elcograf S.p.A.
Subsequently digitally printed in Great Britain

Produced on paper from sustainable forests

Contents

Acknowledgements

My grateful thanks go to Caroline Moore for allowing us to use her prayer for St Aidan's Chapel. Thanks also to Glenys Lewis for patiently typing the script, and to the staff at the public library in Holyhead for their help in confirming the dates of feast days and the lives of the saints.

Prayers and verses attributed to *Gormola Kernewek* (Cornish Praise) are taken from a collection of prayers and poems composed by the author.

Selected Psalms on pages 145–67 are taken from the Book of Common Prayer, the rights in which are vested in the Crown, and are reproduced by permission of the Crown's Patentee, Cambridge University Press.

Bible quotations have been taken from the following sources:

ASB   Alternative Service Book
BCP   Book of Common Prayer
GNB   Good News Bible
KJV   King James Version
NEB   New English Bible
NIV   New International Version
RSV   Revised Standard Version

Foreword

by the Rt Revd William Ind, former Bishop of Truro

When we hear the Bible read in church or read it ourselves at home, it is very easy to miss the fact that most of the great events recorded in Scripture take place not indoors but in the open air. We need to remind ourselves of that constantly – that God is the Lord of all that is and not just a part of life that can be conveniently labelled 'religious'.

The contemporary interest in Celtic spirituality is a real antidote to this narrowing down, and *A Celtic Liturgy* is a real example of it. This book takes Creation seriously and finds God within it. Wind and rain, sun and snow, everyday experiences, all have their part and their place. But this is not nature worship or a book of New Age liturgies, because it is Christocentric and rooted in tradition.

There are services for different times of the day and for other occasions such as the blessing of a marriage or for a funeral. There is also a very useful Celtic calendar, which gives short histories of the saints as well as the saint's day and Bible readings and a collect for each of them.

Some of the material in this book is ancient and some modern, and both are evidence of the rich continuous tradition. Here in Cornwall we are surrounded by physical signs of this tradition, with many Celtic crosses and churches dedicated to Celtic saints. Pat Robson is herself a priest in such a place, and what gives the book an extra dimension and freshness is that the author herself expresses the Celtic tradition by the way she exercises her ministry in her parish and far beyond. There is an openness to all that is, and a sense always that God is here, wherever here is.

+ BILL

Introduction

When Jesus walked on earth and worked among men he was often lonely and tired. The people who crowded around him begging for help gave him no space. He worked late into the night and he felt power leave him when he healed, but his compassion was such that he could not hold back. He found it hard to pace himself in the face of such need. When the crowds were gone to their beds, and only then, tired as he was, he would slip away into the hills to pray alone.

> In prayer Jesus became transformed. He melted
> into God. (Matthew 17:1–5)
> In prayer he was strengthened to continue his
> work. (Mark 1:35)
> In prayer he was comforted and affirmed.
> (Luke 22:39–43)

Like Jesus, when we pray we too become transformed, strengthened, comforted and affirmed. We are 'dipped again in God and new created' (an expression from D.H. Lawrence's poem 'Shadows').

When we try to pray the Celtic way we need to make Christ our friend and talk to him in a very simple manner. It is important not to use words or phrases that we do not understand. It is also important to keep the conversation going.

The Celtic saints prayed by chatting to their loving Saviour as they walked through life. Their favourite prayers, songs and psalms were committed to memory and stored in the treasury of the mind, to be dipped into and drawn upon when needed. The rhythm of a prayer made remembering easy.

The Celtic saints sang their praises to the skies. Knowing the psalms and their chosen prayers by heart, they were saved from poring over books as they worshipped. Modern churchgoers might find their manner crude and oversimplified, but if we want to recreate in some way the naturalness and verve of their worship, we must become less inhibited and avoid any affectations of piety. Instead we should strive to be observant and appreciative of the world around us, wondering and reverent of God's awesome power, and impulsive in love.

The early saints were hard on themselves. They were disciplined and strict about their practices, many of which we would consider very harsh. Despite all this, however, there was no room for religiosity in Christian Celtic spirituality. Affectation and ritual were abhorred. The Eucharist, very simply celebrated and distributed, would have been the only 'formal' service known to them.

For our part, because we are no longer so close to the created world around us, there seems to be a need for a simple liturgy to help us recapture something of the essence of the spirituality of the early Celtic Christians, and that is what this book sets out to provide.

The book will give you some idea of prayers to pray and readings to read, but each moment of prayer will be unique to you as an individual, so revel in the uniqueness of the moment and allow your individuality to make its mark. Different prayers will appeal at different times. Learn the ones you like by rote and speak them from your heart.

It is you who are loved by God. It is your prayers he wants to hear. The form of service is irrelevant. Do not let it become your master.

To help you use this book

Usage

Some of the prayers and services are for the use of individuals praying alone, especially Early Morning Prayer and Night Prayer, and the first section of 'Prayers before Worship' is marked for this purpose. Others are clearly for group use, whether in church or in a more informal setting.

The Caim

The Early Morning Prayer contains a *Caim* (pronounced 'kyme'). The Caim was used by Celtic Christians to create a shield of protection around themselves before they ventured out into the world. With the index finger of the right hand raised and extended, turn clockwise three times, drawing a circle around yourself in the air. As you turn, pray out loud for the protection of the Trinity, the Father, the Son and the Holy Spirit, to keep you safe from harm and to keep you always surrounded by the presence of God.

The Caim is also used in the Service of Healing which occurs later in the book, in order to surround those who are seeking healing with the love and protection of God. If there are several people to be encircled and the space is small, the minister could draw this circle in the air above and towards the people. Alternatively, it may be possible for those who are assisting the minister in the healing to stand around the outside of the group with arms outstretched to form a circle while the words are being said.

Adaptation

All the services can be adapted to suit the occasion, and ministers should feel free to be inventive. Morning Prayer and Evening Prayer, for example, can both be shortened by stopping the service after the Gloria and starting it again with the Lord's Prayer. An asterisk (*) marks the beginning and end of the section which can be left out.

It is always a good idea to encourage as many people as possible to take an active part in the services. The role of the Reader is an important one. He or she keeps the service moving and enables the minister's role to be more sacramental in nature. Where several Readers or Speakers are suggested, as in the Service of Healing, the idea is to encourage people to identify themselves with issues that are important to them. If it is not easy to find enough people, the words can be adapted for use by one Reader only. Likewise, if a reading might be better expressed using more than one Reader, you should feel free to adapt or divide up the material accordingly.

Readings and prayers

The choices of Celtic readings are printed out in full within each service so that it is not necessary to use several books. A Celtic Calendar (pages 96–144) lists relevant saints' days and gives an account of each saint's life which can be read out, together with a collect and suggested Gospel and Psalm readings. The Psalms appointed for each Celtic saint's day can be found in full on pages 145–67.

There are also sections giving a selection of prayers and poems to use before worship (pages 1–7) and in intercessions (pages 83–95). The only other books you may need will be a Bible and a hymn book.

A local language could be used for familar prayers such as the Lord's Prayer if appropriate.

Try to choose hymns to suit the mood and occasion and, if you can do it without unduly lengthening the service, feel free to put in extra hymns where you wish.

Choice of venue

If you are holding any of the services out of doors, be sympathetic to your congregation's needs and provide wind breaks, shelter and seating where necessary. A room or church building which has a simple wild flower decoration, a view from a window or a soft lighting effect can often be just as pleasing and certainly more comfortable for the worshippers than being outside. (If your congregation is determined to worship 'the Celtic way', perhaps they should be encouraged to stand up to their necks in icy water and recite all the Psalms, following the example of St Petroc!)

Blessings

Within the services you will find four kinds of blessing. Each is marked with its own symbol:

✠   marks a point in the service where you may like to sign yourself with a sign of the cross.

✠   marks a point in the service where the minister will individually bless those kneeling before him.

●   marks a point in the service where the minister uses the Orthodox method of blessing, sprinkling holy water three times in the name of Father, Son and Holy Spirit. This occurs in the Service of Marriage but could be used instead of other blessings where preferred.

✝   marks a point in the service where the minister blesses the whole congregation, usually at the end of a service.

I hope you find that the liturgy, prayers and readings stir your imagination and bring you a fresh vision and a real understanding of the God who created you and who loves you so much. God has walked by your side all your life. Why not reach out to him now and speak?

PAT ROBSON

# PRAYERS BEFORE WORSHIP

Praying alone

Dear Lord
The noise and hurry
of the day
have broken their hold
and I have slipped away.

For this small moment in time
I am free
to melt into you.

(Gormola Kernewek)

* * *

My sweet Lord,
Draw me through the darkness
And open my eyes to your wondrous light.

(Gormola Kernewek)

* * *

High King of Heaven,
You stretch out the skies like a curtain
And lower the canopy of gentle night
To cool the heat of the day.
May your peace, dark, velvety and starlit,

Descend
To calm the wild beating of my heart,
That I may be still.

(Gormola Kernewek)

* * *

Let the rumble of traffic diminish
and the song of the birds grow clear
and may the Son of God come striding towards you
walking on these stones.

(Caroline Moore, for St Aidan's Chapel, Bradford Cathedral)

* * *

You are my hiding place O Lord.
You know me by my name.
My thoughts and deeds are seen by you
and their memory brings me pain.

I come to you with a tear-worn soul,
I come to you in grief.

I need the love from your loving heart
That I may be at peace.

Reach out my Lord and touch my soul
And cleanse me from my sin.
Reach out and draw me from the dark
And let your lovelight in.

Your love that fills my soul with joy,
That makes the wild wind sing.
In whiteness, brightness, claim my soul
My loving heavenly King.

(Gormola Kernewek)

Alone with none but you, my God,
I journey on my way.
What need I fear, when you are near,
O King of night and day?
More safe am I within your hand
Than if a host did round me stand.

My life I yield to your command,
And bow to your control,
In peaceful calm, for from your arm
No power can snatch my soul.
Could earthly foes ever appal
A soul that heeds the heavenly call?

(Attributed to St Columba, 6th century)

* * *

Dear, chaste Christ,
Who can see into every heart and read every mind,
Take hold of my thoughts.
Bring my thoughts back to me
And clasp me to yourself.

(Prayer of a Celtic monk, 8th century)

* * *

O Son of God, change my heart.
Your spirit composes the songs of the birds and the
buzz of the bees.
I ask of you only one more miracle:
Beautify my soul.

(Traditional)

Praying together

O God, we thank Thee for this universe our great home; for its vastness and its riches, and for the manifoldness of the life which teems upon it and of which we are part. We praise Thee for the arching sky and the blessed winds, for the driving clouds and the constellations on high.

We praise Thee for the salt sea and the running water, for the everlasting hills, for the trees, and for the grass under our feet. We thank Thee for our senses by which we can see the splendour of the morning, and hear the jubilant song of the birds, taste the autumn fruits, rejoice in the feel of snow and smell the breath of springtime.

Grant us, we pray Thee, a heart wide open to all this joy and beauty, and save our souls from being so steeped in care or so darkened by passion that we pass heedless and unseeing when even the thorn bush by the wayside is aflame with Thy glory.

O God, our creator who livest and reignest for ever and ever.

(Walter Rauschenbusch)

* * *

When we see the simple beauty of the wild flowers in our hedgerows and in our meadows, their colours glowing like jewels among the green summer leaves –

When we see the gulls wheeling high over the cliffs and hear the song of the cuckoo and the meadow lark in the clear morning air –

When we see the butterflies and hear the hum of insects as they hover among the flowers and the tall windblown grasses, and feel the gentle caress of the warm summer breeze –

Then, O Lord, our hearts are raised in joy and thanksgiving, for now the darkness of winter is left behind and the warmth of summer lies ahead.

This beauty, dear Lord, we see as a sign of your love, and we ask that in return you will accept our prayers and our praise, for they come from grateful hearts.

(Gormola Kernewek)

* * *

O Lord, who created the soaring hawk and the raindrop glistening on the bramble leaf, open our eyes to your great glory and set our hearts on fire with your praise.

(Gormola Kernewek)

* * *

Almighty God, we, your people, offer you grateful thanks for this time of refreshment in the midst of our busy lives.

May we, in the quiet and peace of this moment, lay before you ourselves, our hearts, our lives, to do with as you will.

Take from us the cares and worries of our world and let us learn from the beauty we see around us, to trust in your eternal goodness and strength.

Be present among us now as we kneel in
worship.

(Gormola Kernewek)

God is here

Touch the stones
My handsome,
They're steeped in all our prayers.
Touch them with your softness,
Feel the laughter and the tears.
Kneel in quiet
My Robin,
Kneel and add your prayers.
The church is full of memories,
Granite soaked for years.
Kneel in quiet
My Robin,
Kneel
for God is here!

(Gormola Kernewek)

* * *

Green lichen clinging to cut granite stones
Grey sunlight streaming through glass,
Dust dancing on polished oak pews,
Lingering dreams of the past.
Hush as you enter. Walk softly my dear,
Kneel at the altar and pray,
For this is a house where many have come
And where Christ has chosen to stay.

(Gormola Kernewek)

A bud, a flower, a little child – these are the voices that speak to men of God; all that is glad, all that is beautiful, all that is trustful and loving, all that tells of tenderness and constant care – these are Christ's chosen emblems of the Most High.

(Mark Guy Pearse, *Come Break Your Fast*)

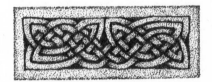

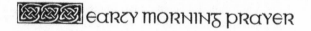# EARLY MORNING PRAYER

Stand to say:

As the morning sun brings light to the world
once more, I come in prayer to you, my Lord. You
created me and you know me. I am your child.

A Psalm may be read.

Kneel to say:

My Father,
I come to you at the beginning of this day
to ask you to guide me and help me.
Give me courage to face the problems that lie
    ahead
and give me a heart wide open to the joys you
    have prepared for me.
Forgive my many sins,
that I may start this day anew.
And as you forgive me,
may I learn to be forgiving and compassionate
    to others in return.
My Father,
I long to serve you aright.
May all that I do and all that I say
be pleasing in your sight.
Amen.

The blessing

I bind unto myself today
The strong name of the Trinity.

(As you say the next three lines you may wish to sign yourself with the sign of the cross.)

✠ The love of the Father who made me,
The love of the Son who died for me,
The love of the Spirit who dwells within me,
Bless me and keep me.
Amen.

The Caim

Stand up and, with the index finger of your right hand raised high, turn clockwise, drawing three circles around yourself, saying:

May the angels of Heaven protect me this day and circle me with the fragrance of peace.
May Christ my Lord and loving friend protect me this day and circle me with affection and love.
May the Spirit of truth who dwells in my heart protect me this day and circle me and fill me with joy.

Stand still

My Father,
I am your child.
I go forth in your name.
Keep me safe.
Amen.

ᛗᚩᚱᚾᛁᛝ ᛈᚱᚪᚣᛖᚱ MORNING PRAYER

Reader
Stand
In the beginning God created the heavens and the earth. Now the earth was formless and empty, darkness was over the surface of the deep, and the Spirit of God was hovering over the waters.

(Genesis 1:1–2 NIV)

Minister
Be thou my vision, O Lord.

All
Be thou my soul's shelter,
O Lord of my heart.

Minister
Eternal God, who knows neither morning nor evening, yet wraps us in love both night and day, Lift the curtain from the world and the veil from our hearts.
Rise with the morning sun upon our souls and enliven our work and prayer.
May we walk this day in the steps of your Son who lived on earth and who always worked in harmony with your will.
Amen.

Reader
And God said, 'Let there be light.'

(Genesis 1:3 RSV)

A candle may be lit.

Sit or kneel

Reader   So God created man in his own image, in the
                  image of God he created him; male and female he
                  created them.
                  (Genesis 1:27 RSV)

                  And God saw everything that he had made, and
                  behold, it was very good.
                  (Genesis 1:31 RSV)

Minister   Secure in the knowledge that God, who created
                  us, loves us dearly, let us now confess before him
                  those sins of which we are ashamed, and which
                  fill our lives with darkness and despair.

                  A short silence may be kept.

All   High King of Heaven, Father of all, in our pride
                  and our weakness we have failed you and we are
                  truly sorry. For the sake of your Son, Jesus Christ
                  our Saviour, who died for us, forgive us our sins
                  and bind us to you with cords of compassion that
                  we may once again walk in the light of your love.

Minister   May the High King of Heaven,
                  With Jesus his Son,
                  Have mercy upon you.
                  May all that dismays you
                  And fills you with fear
                  Be cleansed and forgiven,
                  And in the power of the Spirit
                  May you never be separated
                  From the love of God
                  In Christ Jesus our Lord.
                  Amen.

Minister   O Lord, open our lips.

All   And our mouths shall sing your praise.

Minister   Let us worship the Lord.

All   All praise to his name.

Eternal light shine in our hearts
Eternal goodness deliver us from evil
Eternal power be our support
Eternal wisdom scatter the darkness
of our ignorance.

Eternal pity have mercy on us
That with all our heart and mind
and soul and strength we may seek thy face
and be brought by thine infinite mercy
to thy holy presence.

(Alcuin of York)

Gloria

All   Glory be to the Father and to the Son
And to the Holy Spirit,
As it was in the beginning, is now
And shall be for ever.
Amen.

*Stand

'The creation of the world'

All   *Or the Reader and the congregation could read alternate verses.*

My dear King, my own King, without pride, without sin,
you created the whole world, eternal, victorious King.

King above the elements, King above the sun, King beneath the ocean,
King of the north and south, the east and west, against you no enemy can prevail.

King of the Mysteries, you existed before the elements,
before the sun was set in the sky, before the waters covered the ocean floor;
beautiful King, you are without beginning and without end.

King, you created the daylight, and made the darkness;
you are not arrogant or boastful, and yet strong and firm.

King, you created the land out of shapeless mass,
you carved the mountains and chiselled the valleys,
and covered the earth with trees and grass.

King, you stretched out the sky above the earth,
a perfect sphere like a perfect apple,
and you decorated the sky with stars to shine at night.

King, you pierced the earth with springs from
    which pure water flows,
to form streams and rivers across the land.

King, you ordained the eight winds,
the four primary winds from north and south, east
    and west,
and the four lesser winds that swirl hither and
    thither.

You gave each wind its own colour:
the north wind is white, bringing snow in winter;
the south wind is red, carrying warmth in
    summer;
the west wind is blue, a cooling breeze across the
    sea;
the east wind is yellow, scorching in summer and
    bitter in winter;
and the lesser winds are green, orange, purple and
    black –
the black wind that blows in the darkest nights.

King, you measured each object and each span
    within the universe:
the heights of the mountains and the depths of
    the oceans;
the distance from the sun to the moon, and from
    star to star.

You ordained the movements of every object:
the sun to cross the sky each day, and the moon to
    rise each night;
the clouds to carry rain from the sea, and the
    rivers to carry water back to the sea.

King, you divided the earth into three zones:
the north cold and bitter; the south hot and dry;
and the middle zone cool, wet and fertile.

And you created men and women to be your
        stewards of the earth,
always praising you for your boundless love.

(From *The Celtic Psalter*)

Minister   Let us worship the Lord.

All   All praise to his name.

Sit

First reading

*Taken from the Old Testament or a 'Life' or teaching of
a Celtic saint or teacher (see A Celtic Calendar, pages
96–144).*

Psalm for the day

There should be no pauses mid-verse.
At the end of the Psalm, stand and say together:
Glory to the Father and to the Son
And to the Holy Spirit,
As it was in the beginning, is now
And ever shall be.
Amen.

Sit

Second reading

Taken from the New Testament.

Any of the following may then be read, recited or sung.

'Columba's rock'

Delightful it is to stand on the peak of a rock, in
  the bosom of the isle,
gazing on the face of the sea.

I hear the heaving waves chanting a tune to God
  in heaven;
I see their glittering surf.

I see the golden beaches, the sands sparkling;
I hear the joyous shrieks of the swooping gulls.

I hear the waves breaking, crashing on rocks, like
  thunder in heaven.
I see the mighty whales.

I watch the ebb and flow of the ocean tide; it
  holds my secret,
my mournful flight from Eire.

Contrition fills my heart as I hear the sea; it chants
  my sins,
sins too numerous to confess.

Let me bless almighty God, whose power extends
  over sea and land,
whose angels watch over all.

Let me study sacred books to calm my soul;
I pray for peace, kneeling at heaven's gates.

Let me do my daily work, gathering seaweed,
   catching fish,
giving food to the poor.

Let me say my daily prayers, sometimes chanting,
sometimes quiet, always thanking God.

Delightful it is to live on a peaceful isle, in a quiet
   cell,
serving the King of kings.

(St Columba)

OR

'A hermit's prayer'

Grant me, sweet Christ, the grace to find, Son of
   the Living God
A small hut in a lonesome spot
To make it my abode.

A little pool but very clear, to stand beside the
   place
Where every sin is washed away
By sanctifying grace.

A pleasant woodland all about, to shield it from
   the wind
And make a home for singing birds
Before it and behind.

A southern aspect for the heat, a stream along its
   foot
A smooth green lawn with rich topsoil
Propitious to all fruit.

My choice of those to live with me and pray to
    God as well;
Quiet friends of humble mind
Their number I shall tell.

A lovely church, a home for God, bedecked with
    linen fine,
Where o'er the whitened Gospel page
The Gospel candle shine.

A little house where all may dwell, and body's
    care be sought,
Where none shows lust or arrogance,
None thinks an evil thought.

And all I ask for housekeeping
I get and pay no fees,
Leeks from the garden, poultry, game,
Salmon, fruit and bees.

My share of clothing and of food from the King of
    fairest face,
And I to sit at times alone
And pray in every place.

(Abbot Manteith, 6th century)

OR

'St Ninian's catechism'

Question:	What is best in this world?
Answer:	To do the will of our Maker.
Question:	What is his will?
Answer:	That we should live according to the laws of his creation.

Question: How do we know those laws?

Answer: By study – studying the Scriptures
                with devotion.

Question: What tool has our Maker provided
                for this study?

Answer: The intellect, which can probe
                everything.

Question: And what is the fruit of study?

Answer: To perceive the eternal Word of God
                reflected in every plant and
                insect, every bird and animal, and
                every man and woman.

(St Ninian, 4th/5th century)

The sermon

A hymn may be sung.

Sit or kneel

Prayers and intercessions

Minister   Lord have mercy upon us.

All   Christ have mercy upon us.

Minister   Lord have mercy upon us.*

All   Our Father which art in heaven,
                Hallowed be thy name,
                Thy kingdom come,
                Thy will be done,
                In earth as it is in heaven.

Give us this day our daily bread;
And forgive us our trespasses,
As we forgive them that trespass against us;
And lead us not into temptation,
But deliver us from evil.
For thine is the kingdom, the power, and the glory,
For ever and ever.
Amen.

The minister reads the **Collect for the day** *(from the
Revised Lectionary or from A Celtic Calendar, pages
96–144), followed by* **Prayers and Intercessions
for the world, the sick and the suffering**.

St Columba's prayer

All   Kindle in our hearts, O God,
the flame of love that never ceases,
that it may burn in us, giving light to others.
May we shine for ever in your temple,
set on fire with your eternal light,
even your Son Jesus Christ,
our Saviour and our Redeemer.
Amen.

St Columba's blessing

Minister   See that you are at peace among yourselves,
my children, and love one another.
Take the example of the good men of ancient
times
and God will comfort and aid you,
both in this world and in the world to come.

✝ And the blessing of God almighty,
the Father, the Son and the Holy Spirit,
be among you and remain with you,
now and for ever more.
Amen.

EVENING PRAYER

Stand

Reader The evening mist rises from the ground to refresh
     our souls.
     The birds cease their songs.
     And in the darkening shadows of night, we come
     together in prayer.

Minister Let us worship the Lord.

All All praise to his name.

Reader For the joys and blessings of this day,

Minister let us worship the Lord.

All All praise to his name.

Reader For our Lord Jesus Christ who brought light to the
world,

Minister let us worship the Lord.

All May we walk in his name.

Sit or kneel

Reader The light shines in the darkness and the darkness
has not overcome it.

(John 1:5 RSV)

All   The darkness in our lives brings us grief and our
                 sins are heavy to bear.

Reader   Hear what our Lord says:
                 'Come unto me, all ye that labour and are heavy
                 laden, and I will give you rest.'
                 (Matthew 11:28 KJV)

Minister   When Christ came on earth he lived as a man
                 who knew both hardship and despair.
                 He knows your need.
                 Come to him now and lay your burdens at his feet,
                 and confess those sins of which you are ashamed.

                 A short silence may be kept.

All   Eternal King and Father of all, in our pride and
                 our weakness we have failed you and we are truly
                 sorry. We are ashamed that through our own fault
                 we have brought darkness and misery into the
                 world. For the sake of your Son, Jesus Christ our
                 Saviour, who died for us, forgive us our sins.
                 Illumine the dark corners of our lives with your
                 spirit of light, and kindle once more the flame of
                 your love in our hearts.

Minister   Eternal God, you have lowered the canopy of night
                 and its gentle shadows cover us with your peace.
                 May the dews of heaven heal our wounds and
                 wash the tears from our eyes.
                 And may the burning light of Christ banish for
                 ever the darkness from our souls, that we may be
                 at peace.
                 Amen.

Reader   The people who walked in darkness have seen a
great light.

(Isaiah 9:2 RSV)

A candle may be lit.

All   Eternal light shine in our hearts
Eternal goodness deliver us from evil
Eternal power be our support
Eternal wisdom scatter the darkness
of our ignorance.

Eternal pity have mercy on us
That with all our heart and mind
and soul and strength we may seek thy face
and be brought by thine infinite mercy
to thy holy presence.

(Alcuin of York)

Gloria

All   Glory be to the Father and to the Son
And to the Holy Spirit,
As it was in the beginning, is now
And shall be for ever.
Amen.

*Stand

'The creation of heaven'

All   *Or the Reader and the congregation could read alternate
                 verses.*

King, you created heaven according to your
      delight,
a place that is safe and pure, its air filled with the
      songs of angels.

It is like a strong mighty city, which no enemy can
      invade,
with walls as high as mountains.

It is like an open meadow, in which all can move
      freely,
with people arriving from earth but never leaving.

It is huge, ten times the size of earth,
so that every creature ever born can find a place.

It is small, no bigger than a village,
where all are friends, and none is a stranger.

In the centre is a palace, its walls made of emerald
      and its gates of amethyst;
and on each gate is hung a golden cross.

The roof is ruby, and at each pinnacle stands an
      eagle covered in gold,
its eyes of sapphire.

Inside the palace it is always daylight, and the air
      cool, neither hot nor cold;
and there is a perfect green lawn, with a blue
      stream running across it.

At the edge of this lawn are trees and shrubs,
    always in blossom,
white, pink and purple, spreading a sweet
    fragrance everywhere.

Round the lawn walks a King, not dressed in fine
    robes, but in a simple white tunic,
smiling and embracing those he meets.

And people from outside are constantly entering
    the palace,
mingling one with another, and then leaving.

Everyone in heaven is free to come to the palace,
and then to take with them its perfect peaceful
    joy;
and in this way the whole of heaven is infused
    with the joy of the palace.

(from *The Celtic Psalter*)

Sit

First reading

Taken from the Old Testament or a 'Life' or teaching of a Celtic saint or teacher (see A Celtic Calendar, pages 96–144).

A hymn may be sung.

Psalm for the day

There should be no pauses mid-verse.
At the end of the Psalm stand and say together:

Glory to the Father and to the Son
And to the Holy Spirit,
As it was in the beginning, is now
And ever shall be.
Amen.

Sit

Second reading

Taken from the New Testament.

Any of the following may then be said or sung.

'St Patrick's breastplate'

I bind unto myself today
The strong name of the Trinity,
By invocation of the same,
The Three in One and One in Three.

I bind this day to me for ever,
By power of faith, Christ's Incarnation;
His baptism in the Jordan River;
His death on cross for my salvation;
His bursting from the spicèd tomb;
His riding up the heavenly way;
His coming at the day of doom;
I bind unto myself today.

I bind unto myself the power
Of the great love of the Cherubim;
The sweet 'Well done' in judgement hour;
The service of the Seraphim,
Confessors' faith, Apostles' word,
The Patriarchs' prayers, the Prophets' scrolls.
All good deeds done unto the Lord,
And purity of virgin souls.

I bind unto myself today
The virtues of the starlit heaven,
The glorious sun's life-giving ray,
The whiteness of the moon at even,
The flashing of the lightning free,
The whirling wind's tempestuous shocks,
The stable earth, the deep salt sea,
Around the old eternal rocks.

I bind unto myself today
The power of God to hold and lead,
His eye to watch, His might to stay,
His ear to hearken to my need.
The wisdom of my God to teach,
His hand to guide, his shield to ward;
The word of God to give me speech,
His heavenly host to be my guard.

Against the demon snares of sin,
The vice that gives temptation force,
The natural lusts that war within,
The hostile men that mar my course;
Or few or many, far or nigh,
In every place, and in all hours
Against their fierce hostility,
I bind to me these holy powers.

Against all Satan's spells and wiles,
Against false words of heresy,
Against the knowledge that defiles,
Against the heart's idolatry,
Against the wizard's evil craft,
Against the death-wound and the burning
The choking wave and poisoned shaft,
Protect me, Christ, till thy returning.

Christ be with me, Christ within me,
Christ behind me, Christ before me,
Christ beside me, Christ to win me,
Christ to comfort and restore me,
Christ beneath me, Christ above me,
Christ in quiet, Christ in danger,
Christ in hearts of all that love me,
Christ in mouth of friend and stranger.

I bind unto myself the name,
The strong name of the Trinity;
By invocation of the same.
The Three in One, and One in Three,
Of whom all nature hath creation;
Eternal Father, Spirit, Word:
Praise to the Lord of my salvation,
Salvation is of Christ the Lord.

OR

'Be thou my vision'

Be thou my vision, O Lord of my heart,
Be all else but naught to me, save that thou art;
Be thou my best thought in the day and the night,
Both waking and sleeping, thy presence my light.
Be thou my wisdom, be thou my true word,
Be thou ever with me, and I with thee, Lord;
Be thou my great Father, and I thy true son;
Be thou in me dwelling, and I with thee one.
Be thou my breastplate, my sword for the fight;
Be thou my whole armour, be thou my true
    might;
Be thou my soul's shelter, be thou my strong
    tower;
O raise thou me heavenward, great power of my
    power.
Riches I heed not, nor man's empty praise;
Be thou mine inheritance now and always;
Be thou and thou only the first in my heart;
O sovereign of heaven, my treasure thou art.
High king of heaven, thou heaven's bright sun
O grant me its joys after vict'ry is won;
Great heart of my own heart, whatever befall,
Still be thou my vision, O ruler of all.

(Celtic prayer, translated by Mary Byrne,
versified by Eleanor Hull, 18th/19th century)

OR

'Lord of my heart'

Lord of my heart
Give me vision to inspire me
That, working or resting,
I may always think of you.

Lord of my heart
Give me light to guide me
That, at home or abroad,
I may always walk in your way.

Lord of my heart
Give me wisdom to direct me
That, thinking or acting,
I may always discern right from wrong.

Lord of my heart
Give me courage to strengthen me
That, amongst friends and enemies,
I may always proclaim your justice.

Lord of my heart
Give me trust to console me
That, hungry or well fed,
I may always rely on your mercy.

Lord of my heart
Save me from empty praise
That I may always boast of you.

Lord of my heart
Save me from worldly wealth
That I may always look to the riches of heaven.

Lord of my heart
Save me from military prowess
That I may always seek your protection.

Lord of my heart
Save me from vain knowledge
That I may always study your word.

Heart of my own heart
Whatever befall me
Rule over my thoughts and feelings
My words and actions.

(Ancient Irish)

The sermon

A hymn may be sung.

Sit or kneel

Prayers and intercessions

Minister   Lord have mercy upon us.

All   Christ have mercy upon us.

Minister   Lord have mercy upon us.*

All   Our Father which art in heaven,
Hallowed be thy name,
Thy kingdom come,
Thy will be done,
In earth as it is in heaven.
Give us this day our daily bread;
And forgive us our trespasses,
As we forgive them that trespass against us;
And lead us not into temptation,

But deliver us from evil.
For thine is the kingdom, the power, and the glory,
For ever and ever.
Amen.

The minister reads **the Collect for the day** *(from the Revised Lectionary or from A Celtic Calendar, pages 96–144), followed by* **Prayers and Intercessions for the world, the sick and the suffering.**

'A million miracles'

Reader   O Son of God, perform a miracle for me: change my heart.
You, whose crimson blood redeems mankind, whiten my heart.

It is you who makes the sun bright and the ice sparkle;
you who makes the rivers flow and the salmon leap.

Your skilled hand makes the nut tree blossom, and the corn turn golden;
your spirit composes the songs of the birds and the buzz of the bees.

Your creation is a million wondrous miracles, beautiful to behold.
I ask of you just one more miracle; beautify my soul.

(Traditional)

St Columba's prayer

All   Kindle in our hearts, O God,
the flame of love that never ceases,
that it may burn in us, giving light to others.
May we shine for ever in your temple,
set on fire with your eternal light,
even your Son Jesus Christ,
our Saviour and our Redeemer.
Amen.

The blessing

Minister   Deep peace of the running wave to you
Deep peace of the flowing air to you
Deep peace of the quiet earth to you
Deep peace of the shining stars to you
Deep peace of the Son of peace to you.

God's blessing be yours
And well may it befall you.
Amen.

After worship

This can be said privately or together as a congregation.

Lord may I be wakeful at sunrise
to begin a new day for you;
Cheerful at sunset for having
done my work for you;

Thankful at moonrise and under starshine
   for the beauty of your universe;
And may I add what little may be in me
   to add to your great world.
Amen.

(The Abbot of Greve)

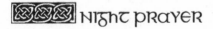 # NIGHT PRAYER

Stand or sit to say:

Here at the end of the day,
in the stillness of the night
I pray.
My Lord, you created me
and you know me.
I am your child.

A Psalm may be read.

Kneel to say:

My Father,
The day is over and the shadows of night fall
    softly round me.
I thank you for the many blessings of the day,
for the people I have met
and the good friends who have helped me on my
    way,
for the special moments of joy which have made
    my heart glad,
and for giving me the opportunity to show your
    love to others.
My Father,
I long to serve you aright.
I am truly sorry for those moments where I failed
    you.

Forgive me,
that I may lie down this night in peace.
Amen.

The blessing

May the peace of the night enfold me,
so that I may be bathed in love.

*(As you say the next three lines you may wish to sign
yourself with the sign of the cross.)*

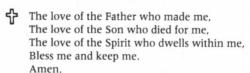 The love of the Father who made me,
The love of the Son who died for me,
The love of the Spirit who dwells within me,
Bless me and keep me.
Amen.

The invocation

May Heaven come close as I sleep this night,
and angels surround me with Christ's pure light.
Amen. Amen.

 a service of marriage

All stand

Reader   Welcome into the presence of the Most High God, the High King of Heaven.

Minister   His Spirit is with us.

All   Amen. Amen.

The congregation sit. The couple should remain standing.

Reader   With the birds of the air and the fish of the sea and all created beings, we are his people.

Minister   He created us and loved us and sealed his love with a sign.

All   All praise to the Lord.

Reader   God said to Noah and his sons, 'I am now making my covenant with you and with your descendants, and with all living beings . . . As a sign of this everlasting covenant . . . I am putting my bow in the clouds. It will be the sign of my covenant with the world. Whenever I cover the sky with clouds and the rainbow appears, I will remember my promise to you and to all the animals that a flood will never again destroy all living beings. When the rainbow appears in the clouds, I will see it and remember the everlasting covenant between me and all living beings on earth. That is the sign of the promise which I am making to all living beings.'

(Genesis 9:8–17 GNB)

Minister Throughout the history of mankind God has given us signs to show us how much he loves us – love so powerful that in our Lord and Saviour Jesus Christ it conquered death itself.

Reader Those between whom there is love shall never really be put asunder – not though flesh divide them, not though seas separate them, not though colour and religion segregate them. For they are one in spirit, and at the end shall be reunited.

All Nothing that is good shall ever die.

At this point the minister blesses the whole congregation.

Minister ◗ Receive the blessing of God which falleth as dew from heaven.

All Thanks be to God.

Minister As we are all united with God in his love, so .... and .... have come together today, surrounded by those who care for them, to ask for God's blessing on the love they have for each other, that it may remain pure and constant throughout the journey of their lives.

Lighting the candles

The three passages marked with an asterisk (*) can be said line for line after the minister, but it would be better if they can be read or spoken as one piece by the couple.

The couple stand before three wreaths of flowers which encircle two small candles and one larger one. Each lights one of the smaller candles in turn, saying:

* This candle that I light is a sign of all that I am.
It burns brightly with the flame of my hopes and dreams.
I offer it to you in love.

The other responds:

* Your hopes and your dreams I will respect and defend,
and from my heart I thank you for this sign of your trust.

Minister .... and ...., you both have your hopes and dreams and you bring to each other all that you have experienced in life and all that has moulded and formed you. Each of you is unique and greatly loved by God.

I ask you now, with all of your friends here present, to join with me in a prayer that we may learn to love God as he loves us, that he may be the treasure of our heart, our vision and our joy.

'Be thou my vision'

*To be sung as a congregational hymn or said as a prayer,
led by the Reader.*

Be thou my vision, O Lord of my heart,
Be all else but naught to me, save that thou art;
Be thou my best thought in the day and the night,
Both waking and sleeping, thy presence my light.
Be thou my wisdom, be thou my true word,
Be thou ever with me, and I with thee, Lord;
Be thou my great Father, and I thy true son;
Be thou in me dwelling, and I with thee one.
Be thou my breastplate, my sword for the fight;
Be thou my whole armour, be thou my true
    might;
Be thou my soul's shelter, be thou my strong
    tower;
O raise thou me heavenward, great power of my
    power.
Riches I heed not, nor man's empty praise;
Be thou mine inheritance now and always;
Be thou and thou only the first in my heart;
O sovereign of heaven, my treasure thou art.
High king of heaven, thou heaven's bright sun
O grant me its joys after vict'ry is won;
Great heart of my own heart, whatever befall,
Still be thou my vision, O ruler of all.

(Celtic prayer, translated by Mary Byrne,
versified by Eleanor Hull, 18th/19th century)

The congregation sit

Minister   The love you have for each other is God's gift to
you both.
The joy in your hearts he shares.
I ask you now, before God, to pledge your love
one to the other.

The vows

The couple hold hands and each says to the other:

* I .... vow that my love for you
.... is strong and true.
Before God, and with his help and strength,
I will care for you in kindness and with a joyful
heart, all my days.
All that I am and all that I have I will share with
you.
And as the stars in the sky and the tides of the sea
are constant and true,
I pledge myself to you in faithfulness and love.

The exchange of rings

A   My ring is a symbol of love never ending.

B   Mine is a circle of our sweet belonging.

The rings are placed on each other's fingers.

A   A circle of gold in joy and in sorrow.

B   A circle of gold today and tomorrow.

*Together the couple take their individual candles and
light the central wedding candle, extinguishing the
smaller candles once the central flame is lit. They hold
the candle together, facing the minister.*

Minister   The flame of your love now burns as one.
May it burn forever,
Warming your hearts,
Lightening your path,
And leading you together
towards the one Eternal Light.
Amen.

*A wreath of flowers is placed on the head or around the
neck of each person by their friends.*

Minister   Thine be the grace of love when in flower.

All   Thine be grace for ever and ever.

Minister   In the presence of the High King of Heaven and
before your family and friends you have entrusted
each other with the dreams of your hearts. You
have exchanged your vows of love and you have
given each other symbols of your belonging. In
the eyes of God, two have become one.

The couple kneel.

Minister   Receive this blessing
in the name of the Father and of the Son, and of
the Holy Spirit.
May the rainbow of many colours bind you to
God himself.

May the soft winds of heaven refresh your spirit
and sunshine brighten your heart.
May the burdens of the day rest lightly upon you.
May God enfold you in love,
and may the blessing of God the Holy Trinity,
bringing peace beyond all understanding,
be with you and remain with you, and all you
love,
now and forever.

All   Amen. Amen.

Minister   .... and ...., your friends have
come here today for you.
Take God's blessing, given so generously to you,
and share it among them all.

*The couple turn, holding the marriage candle between
them, and during the singing of hymns, they may then
circle the congregation, passing on the blessing by word,
touch or smile. They return to stand before the minister
once more.*

Minister   Go forth in the peace of the Lord.

All   Amen. Amen.

Notes for A Service of Marriage

1 **This service is not a legally accepted ceremony of marriage**. It could be used in conjunction with a civil service, or in special cases where permission has been obtained from the registrar. It is primarily a service of commitment to another person.

2 A bowl of clear water to which a chosen aromatic oil has been added should be blessed by the minister before the ceremony begins and used for the two blessings, marked ◆.

3 The blessings should be administered by dipping a bunch of fresh rosemary or heather into the scented water and shaking the droplets three times over the congregation or the couple.

4 The choice of aromatic oil and the flowers used to make the wreaths may reflect something of the hopes and dreams of the couple. Many plants and flowers have traditional meanings, and the following are just some of the possible choices.

> Beech – tolerance
> Blackthorn – courage
> Bluebell – peace
> Buttercup – happiness
> Cherry – confidence
> Frankincense – comfort
> Gentian – happiness
> Geranium – harmony
> Gorse – hope
> Heather – friendship
> Honeysuckle – joy
> Ivy – tenacity
> Jasmine – romance
> Myrrh – healing
> Oak – perseverence
> Orange blossom – lifting the spirits

Primrose – protection
Rose otto – emotional healing
Spikenard – calmness
Star of Bethlehem – serenity
Violet – love
Wild rose – cheerfulness
Ylang ylang – soothing relaxation

5 Hawthorn especially was recognized by the Celts as a symbol of hope and new beginnings. If possible it should be used as part of the general decoration in the church or room where the service is being held.

6 The wreaths for the candles become the wedding crowns later in the service, and should be made by the couple and/or their friends and placed on a suitable table covered by a white cloth.

7 Three white candles, one large and two small, should be placed in the middle of the wreaths.

 # A SERVICE OF GATHERING

(in the Celtic tradition)

*When everyone is gathered, a candle is lit and
a moment of silence is observed.*

Leader   O Lord of our hearts,
Grant us a vision to inspire us.
A mission to enthral us,
And a way of life to delight our souls.

All   Amen.

'Be thou my vision'

Be thou my vision, O Lord of my heart,
Be all else but naught to me, save that thou art;
Be thou my best thought in the day and the night,
Both waking and sleeping, thy presence my light.
Be thou my wisdom, be thou my true word,
Be thou ever with me, and I with thee, Lord;
Be thou my great Father, and I thy true son;
Be thou in me dwelling, and I with thee one.
Be thou my breastplate, my sword for the fight;
Be thou my whole armour, be thou my true might;
Be thou my soul's shelter, be thou my strong tower:
O raise thou me heavenward, great power of my
    power.
Riches I heed not, nor man's empty praise:
Be thou mine inheritance now and always;

Be thou and thou only the first in my heart;
O sovereign of heaven, my treasure thou art.
High king of heaven, thou heaven's bright sun,
O grant me its joys after vict'ry is won;
Great heart of my own heart, whatever befall,
Still be thou my vision, O ruler of all.

(Celtic prayer, translated by Mary Byrne,
versified by Eleanor Hull, 18th/19th century)

Please sit

Leader   To obey God's commands, we must first open our
              eyes to see how precious they are, and sharpen
              our wisdom to discern how sweet they are.
              (Pelagius)

Reader I One of the lawyers came forward and asked
              Jesus, 'Which commandment is first of all?'
              Jesus answered, 'The first is, "Hear O Israel: the
              Lord our God is the only Lord; love the lord your
              God with all your heart, with all your soul, with
              all your mind, and with all your strength." The
              second is this: "Love your neighbour as yourself."
              There is no other commandment greater than
              these.' The lawyer said to him, 'Well said, Master.
              You are right in saying that God is one and
              beside him there is no other. And to love Him
              with all your heart, all your understanding, and
              all your strength, and to love your neighbour
              as yourself – that is far more than any burnt
              offerings or sacrifices.' When Jesus saw how
              sensibly he answered, he said to him, 'You are
              not far from the kingdom of God.'

              (Mark 12:28–34, NEB)

Reader II   There are two kinds of divine command; one
prohibits certain attitudes and actions; the other
enjoins certain attitudes and actions. Thus, for
example, hatred and malice are prohibited; love
and generosity are enjoined. Some people regard
the former kind of law as more important than
the latter; they believe that if they avoid doing
what God prohibits, that will be sufficient for
them to be saved. Indeed many people have
gained the impression that Christianity amounts
to little more than a series of prohibitions. But in
truth the second kind of law is equally important;
indeed the first kind is useless without the second.

A society in which people only avoided certain
actions, but never did anything good, would be
utterly dead; it would be like the valley of dry
bones which the prophet describes. A society can
only live if people love and serve one another.

So when you are aware of hatred in your heart,
do not simply suppress it, but transform it into
love. When you desire to commit a malicious
act, do not simply stop yourself; transform that
act into a generous one.'

(A commentary by the British theologian Pelagius who lived at
the end of the 4th century AD)

Leader   Teach us, good Lord, that your commands to us are
sweeter than honey and more precious than gold.

(Pelagius)

All   Transform our lives, O Lord, and beautify our
souls, that your Church may be a force for good
in the world: full of hope and optimism and joy.

Leader   The Lord who created you says, 'Do not be afraid, you are precious to me and I love you and give you honour.'
(Isaiah 43:1, 4)

All   God our Father, hold us in the hollow of your hand and keep us safe.

Leader   'I am the good shepherd', said Christ, 'and I lay down my life for the sheep.'
(John 10:11, 15, KJV)

All   Teach us of love, O Lord, that we might see the world with your eyes and love with your heart.

Leader   God says, 'I will pour out my spirit on all flesh, your sons and your daughters shall prophesy, your old men shall dream dreams and your young men shall see visions.'
(Joel 2:28, RSV)

All   God, grant us the gift of your Holy Spirit, to inspire us to do great things in your name.

Leader   O Trinity of truth and power, circle us with your love.

All   And give to us, your Church, wisdom, love and peace.

Leader   Eternal God, Creator and Father of us all, we thank you for this wonderful world, for the ever-changing skies, the blessed winds, the earth

beneath our feet and for the people and animals
you have given us to love and share our lives.
Most of all we thank you that your Son gave all
of this life's loveliness in sacrifice for us.

In obedience to your will, and in great humility,
we offer you our lives. All that we do and all that
we say we give in joyful and willing service to
you, our Lord and Heavenly King.

All   Amen.

Leader   We end our service and begin our gathering
               tonight by saying together the prayer of
               St Columba of Iona.

All   Kindle in our hearts, O God.
               The flame of love that never ceases,
               That it might burn in us, giving light to others.
               May we shine for ever in your temple,
               Set on fire with your eternal light,
               Even your Son Jesus Christ,
               Our Saviour and our Redeemer. Amen. Amen.

 # A CELTIC EUCHARIST

Conscious of their diverse backgrounds and increasingly aware of the impermanence of their ways of life as a refugee people, the Celt Christians gained strength from the fact that, in the face of all their problems, God constantly drew them together to share the Eucharist.

Reader   When God pronounced that his creation was good, it was not only that his hand had fashioned every creature; it was that his breath had brought every creature to life. The presence of God's spirit in all living beings is what makes them beautiful.

(Pelagius)

Minister   The Lord is here.

All   His Spirit is with us.

Reader   From the beginning of time, we have travelled from the four corners of the earth to be together for this special moment.

All   The blood of our ancestors flows in our veins and the joy of the saints sings in our hearts.

Reader   Like a shepherd gathers his sheep from the hillside, you have gathered us to this place.

All   For we are your family and you have drawn us to you with bonds of love.

| Minister | Our Lord bids you welcome and invites you all to his table. Come into his presence. Come and join with the saints in Heaven. Come in faith to eat and drink of his body and blood and be at one with him in his suffering and his joy. |

| All | Amen. Amen. |

The Caim

If the group is small, stand in a circle and join hands.

All	May God the Father circle us and keep us safe within his arms.
	May God the Son circle us and fill our hearts with love.
	May God the Holy Spirit circle us and inspire us with his grace.

Eucharistic prayer

| Minister | We thank you our Father for this bread and wine, food and drink to bind us to you in a new covenant: a new agreement, a new beginning. |

| | We thank you for sending us your Son, who gave his life that we might come to you with hearts washed clean by his love. Who, on his last night on earth, at supper with his friends, |

took bread, and when he had given thanks,
he broke it, and gave it to his disciples
saying,

'Take and eat. This is my body, broken for you.
Eat this and remember me.'

All Broken for me, broken for you. Broken for me,
broken for you.

Minister When supper was over he took the cup and
when he had given thanks he said,

'This is my blood of the new covenant given
   for you.
Drink this and remember me.'

All Given for me, given for you. Given for me,
given for you.

Minister Lord Jesus Christ, we remember you with love in
our hearts. We remember your healing presence
on earth, your patient teaching and your acts of
kindness and compassion.

We remember, too, the great dignity you showed
when going to your death and the serenity and
peace with which you proved to your disciples
that death is not the end.

For us, you stepped through the gates of death
and led us into a new life, giving us a new
vision and a new promise and saying,

'Because I live, you will live also' (John 14:19, RSV) and 'I am with you alway, even unto the end of the world' (Matthew 28:20, KJV).

All As we eat and drink of your body and your blood, make us one with each other, and one with you. For we are your people and we long, with all our hearts, to live with you.

Minister *lifting the bread and wine:*
This is God's gift to you. The sign of his great love.
Eat and drink of this together and take Christ into your heart.

After Communion

All Heavenly Father, you have surrounded us by your blessing, dipped us in your love and created us anew in the image of your Son.

May we leave this place with his love in our hearts and go out into the world in his name. May those who meet us on the way, see a little of Christ in all that we do and all that we say, and may we live each moment in joy, sure in the promise that Christ walks with us on the way.

And may the Lord bless us and keep us. The Lord make his face to shine upon us And give us peace.

Minister And may the blessing of God almighty, the
Father, the Son and the Holy Spirit, be with
you and remain with you, always.

All Amen.

All God be in my head, and in my understanding;
God be in my eyes, and in my looking;
God be in my mouth, and in my speaking;
God be in my heart, and in my thinking;
God be at my end, and at my departing.

(Old Sarum Primer)

Minister Go now, and live as Christ in the world.

All Amen, Amen.

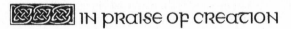 IN PRAISE OF CREATION

A service of thanksgiving and commitment to God

All stand

Reader Behold the kingdom of our Lord.
Behold the beauty of the sky,
the warmth of the earth,
the wonders of his creation.

Minister Come with joy and praise his holy name.

All Amen. Amen.

Reader The Lord who threw stars into space and hung the cobwebs of morning with tears of light, he alone is to be praised.

All Alleluia.

Sit for a **Reading**. *This may be one of the following selection, a Psalm, or a poem chosen or written by a member of the congregation. To truly honour God as Creator we should strive to be creative.*

'Look at the sky'

Look at the sky, how beautiful it is, and how vast, all crowned with a blazing diadem of stars! For how many ages has it existed? Already it has been

there for five thousand years, and shows no signs
of ageing.

Like some young creature full of sap it preserves
all the shining and the freshness of an earlier age,
and manifests the beauty it possessed in the
beginning, and time has not wearied it. And this
vast, beautiful, ageless sky, unchangeable and
gleaming, with all its stars, having existed through
so many ages – this same God, who some profess
to be able to see with mortal eyes and
comprehend with their own pitiable intelligence –
this same God created it as easily as a man,
throwing a handful of sticks together, creates a
hut. And this is what Isaiah meant when he said,
'He stretches out the heavens as a curtain, and
spreadeth them out as a tent to dwell in.'

Look at the great mass of the mountains, and all
the innumerable people who dwell on earth, and
the plants, all so rich and wonderfully varied, and
the towns and the vast buildings and the wild
animals, and all these the earth supports easily
on her back. And yet with all its vastness, it was
fashioned by God 'as though it were nothing'. So
speaks for us Isaiah, searching for a phrase which
will explain the ease with which God created the
earth . . . And then look at the inhabitants of
earth, of whom the prophet said, 'He sitteth upon
the circle of the earth, and the inhabitants thereof
are as grasshoppers,' and a little while earlier he
said, 'Behold the nations are as a drop of water
falling from a bowl.' Think of all the peoples who
inhabit the earth: Syrians, Cilicians, Cappadocians,
Bithynians, those who live on the shores of the

Black Sea, in Thrace, in Macedonia, in all of
Greece and the islands of Britain, Sarmatia, India
and in inhabitants of Persia, and then of all the
innumerable other peoples and races, and all
these are 'as a drop of water falling from a bowl'.
And what small atom of this drop of water thinks
he can know God?

(St John Chrysostom, *De Incomprehensibili*, II, 6, 4th century)

OR

'I have a hut'

I have a hut in a wood: only my Lord knows it; an
    ash tree closes it on one side,
and a hazel like a great tree by a rath on the other.

The size of my hut, small, not too small, a
    homestead with familiar paths.
From its gable a she-bird sings a sweet song in her
    thrush's cloak.

A tree of apples of great bounty like a mansion,
    stout:
a pretty bush, thick as a fist, of small hazel nuts,
    branching and green.

Fair white birds come, herons, seagulls, the sea
    sings to them, no mournful music:
brown grouse from the russet heather.

The sound of the wind against a branching wood,
    grey cloud, river-falls,
the cry of the swan, delightful music!

Beautiful are the pines which make music for me
  unhindered:
through Christ I am no worse off at any time than
  you.

Though you relish that which you enjoy
  exceeding all wealth,
I am content with that which is given me by my
  gentle Christ.

With no moment of strife, no din of combat such
  as disturbs you,
thankful to the Prince who gives every good to me
  in my hut.

(Early Irish lyric, 10th century)

A hymn may be sung. Remain standing after the hymn.

Reader When God pronounced that his creation was
good, it was not only that his hand had fashioned
every creature; it was that his breath had brought
every creature to life. The presence of God's spirit
in all living beings is what makes them beautiful;
and if we look with God's eyes, nothing on earth
is ugly.

(Pelagius)

Minister At our baptism we became sons and daughters of
the High King of Heaven, disciples of his Son our
Lord and Saviour Jesus Christ, and inheritors of
the kingdom of heaven. We join together in a
declaration of our faith.

Speaker I   Eternal God, Creator and Father of us all, when your Son Jesus Christ our Lord came to earth he showed us by his many acts of caring that you are a compassionate and loving God.

All   Open our eyes, O Lord, that we may see you more clearly.

Speaker II   Eternal God, Creator and Father of us all, when your Son Jesus Christ our Lord came to earth he taught us your love with words of wisdom and understanding.

All   Open our ears, O Lord, that we might hear you more clearly.

Speaker III   Eternal God, Creator and Father of us all, when your Son Jesus Christ our Lord came to earth he welcomed all who came to him, the rich and the poor, the Jew and the Gentile, the righteous and the sinner.

All   Open our hearts, O Lord, that we might recognize men and women of all races, colours and creeds as our brothers and sisters, and learn to love without discrimination and fear.

Speaker IV   Eternal God, Creator and Father of us all, when your Son Jesus Christ our Lord came to earth he gave his life on a cross of shame, that we might be free.

All   Open the doorway of our souls, O Lord, that our Saviour may enter and we may be at peace.

Speaker V   Eternal God, Creator and Father of us all, on a
glorious morning three days after his crucifixion
your Son Jesus Christ defied the darkness of death
and rose again to a new life.

All   Open our minds, O Lord, to this wonderful truth,
that we may live our lives without fear, trusting in
your word and rejoicing always in your
faithfulness.

Reader   And Jesus said to those who followed him: 'This is
my commandment: love one another, as I have
loved you. There is no greater love than this, that
a man should lay down his life for his friends. You
are my friends, if you do what I command you.
I call you servants no longer; a servant does not
know what his master is about. I have called you
friends, because I have disclosed to you everything
that I heard from my Father.
  You did not choose me: I chose you. I appointed
you to go on and bear fruit, fruit that shall last; so
that the Father may give you all that you ask in
my name. This is my commandment to you: love
one another.'

(John 15:12–17 NEB)

Minister   Eternal God, Creator and Father of us all,
We thank you for this wonderful world, for the
ever-changing skies, the blessed winds and the
earth beneath our feet. And we thank you that
your Son gave all of this life's loveliness in
sacrifice for us. In our turn, and in great humility,
we offer our lives. All that we do and all that we
say we give in joyful and willing service to you,
our Lord and Heavenly King. Amen.

'St Patrick's breastplate'

To be sung as a hymn or chanted all together.

I bind unto myself today
The strong name of the Trinity,
By invocation of the same,
The Three in One and One in Three.

I bind this day to me for ever,
By power of faith, Christ's Incarnation;
His baptism in the Jordan River;
His death on cross for my salvation;
His bursting from the spicèd tomb;
His riding up the heavenly way;
His coming at the day of doom;
I bind unto myself today.

I bind unto myself the power
Of the great love of the Cherubim;
The sweet 'Well done' in judgement hour;
The service of the Seraphim,
Confessors' faith, Apostles' word,
The Patriarchs' prayers, the Prophets' scrolls.
All good deeds done unto the Lord,
And purity of virgin souls.

I bind unto myself today
The virtues of the starlit heaven,
The glorious sun's life-giving ray,
The whiteness of the moon at even,
The flashing of the lightning free,
The whirling wind's tempestuous shocks,
The stable earth, the deep salt sea,
Around the old eternal rocks.

I bind unto myself today
The power of God to hold and lead,
his eye to watch, his might to stay,
His ear to hearken to my need.
The wisdom of my God to teach,
His hand to guide, his shield to ward;
The word of God to give me speech,
His heavenly host to be my guard.

Against the demon snares of sin,
The vice that gives temptation force,
The natural lusts that war within,
The hostile men that mar my course;
Or few or many, far or nigh,
In every place, and in all hours
Against their fierce hostility,
I bind to me these holy powers.

Sit for a **Reading from the Gospels**.

The sermon

Minister Let us pray.

All Christ be with me, Christ within me,
Christ behind me, Christ before me,
Christ beside me, Christ to win me,
Christ to comfort and restore me,
Christ beneath me, Christ above me,
Christ in quiet, Christ in danger,
Christ in hearts of all that love me,
Christ in mouth of friend and stranger.

I bind unto myself the name,
The strong name of the Trinity;
By invocation of the same.
The Three in One, and One in Three,
Of whom all nature hath creation;
Eternal Father, Spirit, Word:
Praise to the Lord of my salvation,
Salvation is of Christ the Lord.

All stand

*Those wishing to make a commitment to God should step
forward and make their promise, choosing the most
appropriate phrase from those listed below, or creating a
new form of words. Each person in turn says:*

I .... wear this ring or cross,
[or] I......... undertake to ....,
[or] I......... offer my skills as a .... to ....,
as a token of my love,
and I offer myself in service to you,
my Lord and Heavenly King.

All   Alone with none but you, my God,
I journey on my way.
What need I fear, when you are near,
O King of night and day?
More safe am I within your hand
Than if a host did round me stand.

My life I yield to your command,
And bow to your control,
In peaceful calm, for from your arm
No power can snatch my soul.

Could earthly foes ever appal
A soul that heeds the heavenly call?

(Prayer of St Columba)

Minister   *(to each person in turn)*
✠   Receive the sign of the cross.

(to all)
This is to show that you have given your lives in
service to God. Wear this sign with pride, and
when times are hard and all seems lost, remember
Jesus died, but now he lives.

A moment of silence may be kept.

Reader   You who work by Christ's side
And share his great love,
You who touch with his hands
And feel with his heart,
His blessing is yours,
His joy till the end.
Take it.
Hold it.
You are his friend.

(Gormola Kernewek)

A moment of silence may be kept.

The blessing

Minister   May God the Father hold you in the palm of his
✝   hand and keep you from harm.

May Jesus his Son walk by your side along the
way.
May his Holy Spirit of fire quicken your hearts
and keep you faithful and true,
and when the gates of death open may you put
your hand into the hand of our Lord
and step with joy into the court of the High King
of Heaven himself,
and may you be at peace.
Amen.

*The service should end on a note of celebration, with
singing, dancing or feasting, and in joyous thanksgiving.*

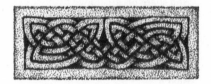

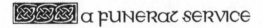 a funeral service

All stand

Minister   The Lord bless you and keep you:
The Lord make his face to shine upon you, and be
gracious to you:
The Lord lift up his countenance upon you, and
give you peace.

(Numbers 6:24–6 RSV)

Reader I   As the gentle breeze of springtime warms our
winter world,
a new year begins.
As the golden sun of morning scatters the
shadows of night,
a new day begins.
As our Lord Jesus Christ reaches out to take our
hand at the gate of death,
so a new life begins.

Minister   Let us pray.
Dear Lord and Heavenly Father, we thank you for
giving us .... to live among us and to
touch our lives with *his/her* loving presence. We
his/her family and friends who loved *him/her*
dearly are gathered here to give *him/her* back to
you whose love for *him/her* is greater than ours
can ever be. We stand here at the beginning of
his/her new life to send *him/her* forth surrounded
by our love. Increase our faith and comfort our

sorrow, and allow your peace to fill our hearts. We
ask this in the name of Jesus Christ our Lord.
Amen.

A hymn may be sung.

Sit

Reader I   This present sorrow has awakened in us many
doubts and fears.
In our weakness give us strength, O Lord.
In our doubt give us faith.

Reader II   Jesus said, 'Let not your heart be troubled: ye
believe in God, believe also in me. In my Father's
house are many mansions: if it were not so, I
would have told you. I go to prepare a place for
you. And if I go and prepare a place for you, I will
come again, and receive you unto myself; that
where I am, there ye may be also.'
(John 14:1–3 KJV)

Reader I   When our Lord Jesus Christ made this promise,
he knew that his own death was not far away. He
could have avoided the conflict. Even on the last
evening when the disciples were all asleep and
Jesus was alone in the Garden of Gethsemane,
he could have melted into the shadows and run
away. Instead he chose to stay and meet death
face to face, so that we could see his promise to us
come true; so that we need never be afraid again.

Reader II   So God loved the world, that he gave his only-
begotten Son, to the end that all that believe in
him should not perish, but have everlasting life.

(John 3:16 ASB)

Minister   Let us pray.
Dear Lord and Heavenly Father, we thank you
that your Son, our Lord and Saviour Jesus Christ,
gave up this life's loveliness for us and opened the
gates of heaven itself, that we might go in. Eternal
God, hold us in the hollow of your hand.

All   Keep us as the apple of your eye.

The eulogy

Giving praise for the gift of life.

*A moment of silence could be kept, so that those present
may say their own personal goodbyes to the deceased.*

A hymn may be sung.

The Lord's Prayer could be said together.

*The congregation may wish to stand for the
commendation and committal.*

The commendation

Minister   Receive, Lord, in tranquillity and peace the soul of
.... who has departed this present life to be

with you. We who loved *him/her* commend
him/her to you. Forgive *him/her his/her* sins. Give
him/her the life that knows no age, the good things
that do not pass away, and accept *him/her* with
unconditional love into your kingdom, where
light perpetual shines and where *he/she* may be at
peace.

Pause

Go forth, O Christian soul, in the name of God
who knows you and with the blessing of those
who love you.

The committal

Minister   Sure in the promise of our Lord Jesus Christ and
trusting in the grace and compassion of God, we
now commit *his/her* body *to the ground/to be
cremated*. Eternal God who scatters the stars into
the blackness of space, who watches when the
smallest sparrow falls, who knows the wonder of
joy and the agony of despair, and who delights in
all that he has made, we give our loved one into
your care.

Reader I   Jesus said, 'Peace I leave with you, my peace I
give unto you. Let not your heart be troubled,
neither let it be afraid.'
(John 14:27 KJV)

Reader II   'Lo, I am with you alway, even unto the end of
the world.'

(Matthew 28:20 KJV)

The blessing

Minister   May the light of Christ pierce the darkness of your
✝   grief.
May the love of Christ lift your spirits and gladden
each day.
May the peace of Christ fill your hearts and
comfort your sorrow.
May Christ our Saviour walk by your side, today
and tomorrow.
And may the blessing of our Eternal God and
Father be with you, now and until the ages of
ages.
Amen.

 # a service of healing

Stand

Reader My dear King, my own King, without pride, without sin,
you created the whole world, Eternal victorious King.

King of the Mysteries, you existed before the elements,
before the sun was set in the sky, before the waters covered the ocean floor;
beautiful King, you are without beginning and without end.

High King, you created the daylight, and made the darkness;
you are not arrogant or boastful, and yet strong and firm.

Eternal King, you created land out of the shapeless mass,
you carved the mountains and chiselled the valleys,
and covered the earth with trees and grass.

King and Father of all, you created men and women to be your stewards of the earth,
always praising you for your boundless love.

(Adapted from 'The creation of the world', from *The Celtic Psalter*)

Sit or kneel

All   High King of Heaven and creator of all,
                we your people confess our weakness before
                you.
            Where you are humble and free of sin,
                we are proud and sinful.
            Where you are strong and firm,
                we are arrogant and boastful.
            Because of our weakness,
                the world is suffering.

Minister   Lord, hear the suffering of your people.

Speaker I   I speak for all the peoples of the world, the victims
                of war and disaster, and all those who are hurt or
                hungry, afraid or anxious.
                Lord in your compassion,

All   come near to heal and to bless.

Speaker II I speak for the earth itself – how it groans as
                mankind despoils its beauty and is careless of its
                natural laws!
                Lord in your compassion,

All   come near to heal and to bless.

Speaker III I speak for all animals and birds and for all
                creatures that are frightened or in pain because of
                human carelessness and cruelty.
                Lord in your compassion,

All   come near to heal and to bless.

Speaker IV   I speak for the children who are abandoned or lost, without families and without love, for those who live on the streets, for those who live in institutions, for all children everywhere who are abused, frightened or alone.
Lord in your compassion,

All   come near to heal and to bless.

Speaker V   I speak for all those who are sick, those who are in pain, those waiting for surgery, those who face long-term illnesses or incurable diseases.
Lord in your compassion,

All   come near to heal and to bless.

Speaker VI   I speak for all those people who are homeless or unemployed and all those anxious about money.
Lord in your compassion,

All   come near to heal and to bless.

Speaker VII   I speak for all people who have lost control of their lives and who are dependent upon drink and drugs.
Lord in your compassion,

All   come near to heal and to bless.

Speaker VIII   I speak for all who are sick and those known to us who are in need of help.
Lord in your compassion,

All   come near to heal and to bless.

Minister   Let us pray.
Dear Lord and Heavenly Father, we live in a world
where much is amiss and we are ashamed of the
part we have played in spoiling your creation and
causing you pain.

All   We confess that we have been careless of the gifts
you have given us, selfish and indifferent towards
other people, and above all we have been
neglectful of our relationship with you. We are
ashamed and heartily sorry, and in knowledge
of your enduring compassion we beg you to
forgive us.

Minister   May God the Father who created you and who
knows your innermost thoughts wash away your
sins and give you new life.
May God the Son who walks by your side and
who shares your sorrows and your joys look with
compassion upon all your doings.
May God the Holy Spirit who inspires mankind
with the power and goodness of God fill your lives
with hope and with love, that you may walk for
ever in the radiant brightness of the High King of
Heaven in peace and in joy.
Amen.

First reading

Mark 1:21–45

Reader   See where he walks
With love in his face.
The sick
They touch his hem.
He looks so tired
And yet he loves.
Dear of him.
He weeps for you
He weeps for me.
Dear my Lord
He weeps.

(Gormola Kernewek)

Minister   We light a candle for those who suffer.

A candle is lit.

O Lord, kindle a flame in our hearts,

All   that we may show your compassion in the world
and that through us Christ may walk on earth
once more.

Reader   Christ has no body on earth but yours
No hands but yours
No feet but yours
Yours are the eyes through which Christ's
compassion is to look out for the world
Yours are the feet with which he is to go about
doing good

Yours are the hands with which he is to bless us
now.

(Teresa of Avila, 16th century)

A hymn may be sung.

Sit

Second reading

Acts 3:1–10

All   We are all children of the same Heavenly Father.
            We all have a mission in life, a task that is for us
                  alone.
            We all know what it is to have joy in our hearts.
            Help us to learn that our joys have a purpose.
            We all know what it is to suffer.
            Help us to learn that our sufferings have a
                  purpose.

Minister   We are all in the hands of God.
            He will help us bear the pain,
            and in the fullness of time
            he will bring us into the light of a new day,
            new born and whole once more.

            *Those who have come for personal healing should kneel
            at the altar rail, or sit or kneel surrounded by the
            congregation.*

Reader   We open the roof
to lay our loved ones
at your feet.

Great King
Surround them with
the shining presence
of your love.

Loving Saviour
Heal their hurts
with your
tender touch.

Spirit of Fire
Give them
new life!

(Gormola Kernewek)

All   Our Father which art in heaven,
Hallowed be thy name,
Thy kingdom come,
Thy will be done,
In earth as it is in heaven.
Give us this day our daily bread;
And forgive us our trespasses,
As we forgive them that trespass against us;
And lead us not into temptation,
But deliver us from evil.
For thine is the kingdom, the power, and the
glory,
For ever and ever.
Amen.

The Caim

Minister   We draw a circle of love around you all, to keep
              you from harm.
              In the name of the Father who bore you;
              In the name of the Son who loves you;
              In the name of the Spirit who lives in you;
              Receive the protection of the Trinity of power.

All or   *to each person in turn:*
Minister *We/I* lay *our/my* hands upon you in the name of
              our Lord and Saviour Jesus Christ. Receive this
              healing touch and trust in his power.

              *As the people return to their seats, a hymn or hymns
              may be sung.*

              Sit or kneel.

Minister Let us pray.

All   O Lord and Heavenly Father,
              We thank you for your compassion towards us
              and we trust ourselves into your loving care.
              Where we are weak give us strength.
              Where we lack faith fill us with confidence.
              Where we are cold open our hearts to your dear
                Son,
              that he may enter to heal our wounds
              and to be our sweet companion,
              all the days of our life,
              now and for ever.
              Amen.

The blessing

Minister May God's blessing surround you
And love fill your hearts
May Christ walk beside you
And never depart
Holy Spirit keep you faithful
And strong to the end
As the stars light your pathway
Sweet blessings descend.

(Gormola Kernewek)

▨▨▨ PRAYERS OF INTERCESSION

These prayers are not Celtic in origin. They are designed to be used today. The prayers should be directed to God and you may wish to address him as Eternal God, Heavenly Father, High King of Heaven, or Lord. Your own prayers will be more suitable, but there may be occasions when you need a little help and a place from which to start.

The Church

We pray for the family of the Church.

We pray for your Church throughout the world, that it may be filled with the wine of new life and the fire of the Holy Spirit.

Kindle in the hearts of all thy people such love towards you that it wells up and spills over into the life of the world.

May openness and love take the place of hypocrisy and hate.

May generosity and gentleness take the place of greed and aggression, and may the whole world come to know of your love and compassion through the work of a loving and compassionate Church.

Amen.

The Church family

We pray for your Church throughout the world, for all those who have been washed in your love and who strive to follow the teaching of your Son, Jesus Christ our Lord.

Heavenly Father, give to us all a quiet understanding and a will to reach out to each other in compassion. May we be mindful of others' opinions, but delighting always in the wonderful diversity of gifts we each bring to your family. And may we never forget that the world sees you in all that we do and all that we say.

Amen.

Church leaders

We pray for all bishops, priests and deacons and for all who hold positions of authority in your Church.

Guide, we pray you, the thoughts and words of all your servants entrusted with the care of your people. May compassion and love rule in their hearts and be evident in their lives. May they reach out with your arms to the world and bring comfort to your people.

Amen.

*   *   *

We pray for the Church throughout the world.

Dear Lord and Heavenly Father, we pray that you will fill our Church leaders with strength and give them the courage to speak your word and live your gospel in the face of all opposition. Be with all those who hold positions of responsibility in your Church. May they be resolute in their compassion and unwavering in their search for justice, and may they always show your love as light in the world of darkness.

Amen.

*   *   *

Eternal God, we pray for all ministers of the Church.

We pray for your Church and for all priests and people who are keeping alive the gospel of your Son, our Lord Jesus Christ, in the parishes and communities throughout the world. In times of loneliness and weariness cheer them with your presence, in disappointment give them patience, in failure give them strength to persevere, and at all times deepen in them the sense of dependence upon you and give them peace in your service.

Amen.

Those who have died

Heavenly Father, help us to entrust our loved ones to thy care. When sorrow darkens our lives, teach us to look up to thee, remembering the cloud of witnesses by whom we are encompassed. And grant that we on earth, rejoicing ever in thy presence, may share with them the rest and peace which thy presence gives.

Amen.

* * *

O Father of all, we pray to thee for those we love but see no longer. Grant them thy peace. Let light perpetual shine upon them, and in thy loving wisdom and almighty power work in them the good purpose of thy perfect will.

Amen.

Those in distress

We remember:
Those who are ill or in pain and who find it hard to get through each day.

Those who are nearing the ending of their days on earth.
Those who have been parted by death from the ones they love.
Those who have lost the ones they love, parted by misunderstanding and hate.
Those who live alone and who are desperately lonely.
Those who are abused and who live their lives in fear and shame.
Those for whom there is no food and who are dying of hunger.

Heavenly Father, be with these and all who are in distress. Give us strength to join you in your work and labour by your side until your kingdom comes on earth and all people see your glory.
    Amen.

Education

We pray for those who are responsible for the upbringing and education of children, that both parents and teachers may be able to give them a desire to explore the world of knowledge, a sense of the wonder of life, and the ability to embrace what is good and to reject what is evil.
    Make us strong in spirit to serve you in our learning so that our children and generations still to come will learn to know you still more clearly and love you yet more dearly.
    Amen.

The elderly

We pray for all elderly people, especially for those who are housebound or lonely, those who are ill or unable to get about as they once could, those who find it difficult to make ends meet and those who find it hard to keep up with the rush and bustle of life today.

Eternal God, grant them good memories and good friends to care for them, and may their remaining years be years of peace and dignity.
Amen.

Evening prayers

Come close to our hearts this evening and listen to our prayers. Let us feel your presence ever near us as we lay our burdens at your feet and offer our souls to your service.
Amen.

* * *

Show your loving kindness to all of us tonight, O Lord, for we all stand in need of your help. Be with the weak to make them strong, and with the strong to make them gentle. Cheer the lonely with your company and the worried with your peace. Prosper the Church in the fulfilment of her mighty task and grant your blessing to all who have toiled in Christ's name.
Amen.

* * *

Watch, dear Lord, with those who wake or watch or weep tonight and give your angels charge over those who sleep. Tend your sick ones, O Lord, rest your weary ones, bless your dying ones, soothe your suffering ones, shield your joyous ones, and all for your love's sake.
Amen.

Faith

When your Son lived on earth he gathered the children into his arms and rejoiced in the simplicity of their faith. Give us such faith, that we who are bowed down by doubts and fears may know, deep in our hearts, the truth of your love, and with the children be ready to accept the wonder and mystery of faith without seeking always to understand.

Amen.

Family

We remember before you, O Lord, our families and our friends. What happens to each of them matters so much to us all. Help us to realize that we share this concern with you and that your love for each of them is greater than ours can ever be. Dear Lord, hold them close to your heart and keep them safe, and may they find comfort in your loving presence.

Amen.

* * *

We remember before you, O Lord, our families and our friends. We hold before you their longings and hopes for the future and their pains of the past, and we ask that you are present with them each day of their lives, teaching them surely but gently of your everlasting love.

Amen.

Governments

Guide all those elected to positions of authority in the world. In their power grant them humility, that they may make wise and compassionate decisions and govern the people with justice and with peace.
　　Amen.

Harvest

We give you hearty thanks for your goodness and loving kindness to us and to all mankind.
　　We thank you for the wonderful summer weather when the crops in our fields grow in abundance, and we thank you that our harvest is safely gathered in now that the storms of autumn have begun.
　　We ask for your continued blessing on all those who work the land, and we ask especially that you bless the people in lands where the crops have failed this year.
　　Through the work of your faithful people may your loving presence be felt in the world and all your people gathered into the harvest of your kingdom.
　　Amen.

The homeless

When your son Jesus Christ lived among us as an ordinary man, he shared with us the loves, the joys and the sadness of family life.
　　He knew what it was to work hard, and when he left his home and his family to do work he chose to live as one who had nowhere to lay his head.

We pray for all those this day who are homeless, for the abandoned children on the streets, for the mentally ill people whom no one wants, for the young people who can no longer live in the family home, for those who have no money.

We pray especially for those who are being exploited, for those who are turning to drink or drugs for consolation, for those who are desperately miserable and who long for a family and a home of their own.

Guard them all, dear Lord, as a shepherd guards his sheep, and when they are ready to receive your help may we be there to open the door and welcome them home.

Amen.

The lonely

We bring to you in our prayers all lonely people, especially those who are too old or infirm to enjoy company and those who are isolated from others through distance, social prejudice, misunderstanding or illness. We pray that friends or neighbours be enabled to reach them and lift them out of their loneliness and bring them comfort and hope. In your mercy, dear Lord, let them feel the warmth of your loving arms around them, for your tender mercy's sake.

Amen.

* * *

We remember how your Son took the lonely road to Jerusalem to face hardship and death. We remember that his followers shouted for joy and did not share his sorrow.

Dear Lord, you who understand all about loneliness even in the midst of joy – be with each one of us here today, for there are many times in our lives when we feel alone and afraid.

Give us the courage to stand up to be counted.

Give us the courage to stand fast to our faith, even in the face of opposition and ridicule.

Teach us how to trust in you and in your love, that we may never be alone again.

Amen.

Meetings

Before

O Lord, we meet in your name and we ask most humbly that your spirit of wisdom and understanding may direct and rule our hearts, that all that we do and all we say may be to your glory and the furtherance of your kingdom, and that in all things we may be faithful servants of your Son, our Saviour Jesus Christ.

Amen.

Before and after

O Lord, we offer you the thoughts and deliberations of this meeting, and we ask that you forgive our shortcomings and our lack of understanding.

May we be mindful of your trust and ready always to work in harmony with each other, that through us your kingdom may go forward and your will be done.

Amen.

Music

O God, Creator of light, of beauty and of joy, we thank you for the gift of music and we offer our voices to your praise. May our songs stir the spirit of worship in our hearts, that we may feel your presence ever near us.
   Amen.

Peace and justice

Be with those who labour for peace and who believe in justice.
   Be with those who fight for what they believe in and for those who suffer because of the fighting.
   And may all people everywhere live in unity and love.
   Amen.

* * *

To you, Creator of nature and humanity, of truth and beauty, I pray:
   Hear my voice, for it is the voice of the victims of all wars and violence among individuals and nations.
   Hear my voice, when I beg you to instil into the hearts of all human beings the wisdom of peace, the strength of justice and the joy of fellowship.
   Hear my voice, for I speak for the multitudes in every country and in every period of history who do not want war and are ready to walk the road of peace.
   Amen.

(Pope John Paul II)

The persecuted

Eternal God, we call upon you,
    for those who are persecuted, exploited and marginalized,
    for political detainees and for people who have 'disappeared',
and for their families,
    for tribal people whose culture and livelihood are under
attack,
    for urban workers, for small farmers, who feel they are fight-
ing a losing battle to feed their children,
    for women forced by poverty to sell their bodies,
    for children who live on the streets with no family love to
support them,
    for the countless thousands of unwanted, nameless souls who
are trapped in gaunt state institutions and who will never know
what it is to run through fields of flowers.
    We pray that one day the candle of your love shining in the
darkness of their lives will bring them peace and that in justice
and mercy your kingdom will indeed be established here on
earth.
    Amen.

Recession

In this time of recession we remember all those who have finan-
cial problems and are finding life difficult.
    We hold before you, O Lord, all those who are fearful for
their jobs, all those who are desperately looking for work and
all those who have become depressed and have given up
looking.
    May your Holy Spirit come among us to heal the tensions of
this time and calm the many fears.

And with Christ by our side, make us aware of each other's troubles so that we may reach out our hands with his friendship and give unstintingly of his love.

Amen.

The prayer of St Francis

Lord, may we be instruments of your peace.
Where there is hatred may we sow love.
Where there is injury, pardon.
Where there is doubt, faith.
Where there is despair, hope.
Where there is darkness, light.
Where there is sadness, joy.
O Divine Master, grant that we may not so much seek
to be consoled as to console;
to be understood as to understand;
to be loved as to love.
For it is in giving that we receive;
It is pardoning that we are pardoned;
And it is in dying that we are born to eternal life.

Amen.

Service

Almighty God our Heavenly Father, whose Son taught us that every service done for others' sake is done for him: give us the wisdom, the will and the strength to be living examples of this truth, that in serving one another we may be glorifying him, our Saviour and our Lord.

Amen.

The sick

O God our Father, Creator of all mankind, you made us in your image and you are glad in our happiness and sad in our misery. We remember before you all those who are sick, all those in pain and all those who are afraid.

Be with them and all those who care for them, and may the Holy Spirit of your presence surround them with your love and inspire them with your strength and give them comfort and peace.

In their pain give relief, in their tiredness give rest and, if it be thy will, restore them to health and fill their lives with joy.

Amen.

Tolerance

Grant us the grace to be sensitive to the dreams and feelings of those around us, and give to each one of us the desire to work together to build your kingdom here on earth and so make this world a place where mankind can live together in the everlasting joy of your love.

Amen.

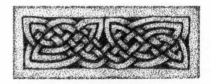

 A CELTIC CALENDAR

Calendar of Celtic saints

17 January	St Antony of Egypt
1 February	St Brigid
14 February	St Adwenna
1 March	St David
2 March	St Chad
5 March	St Piran
9 March	St Constantine *(11 March in Scotland)*
17 March	St Patrick
20 March	St Cuthbert
27 April	St Enoder
28 April	St Guenole
1 May	St Brioc
5 May	St Gwinear
16 May	St Carantoc *(26 May in Wales)*
4 June	St Petroc
7 June	St Meriadoc
9 June	St Columba
15 June	St Non
28 July	St Samson
31 August	St Aidan
16 September	St Ninian
3 October	St Kea
10 October	St Paul Aurelian
17 October	St Levan
27 October	St Ia *(originally 3 February; 18 September in Brittany)*
6 November	St Illtyd
8 November	St Cuby
11 November	St Martin
17 November	St Hilda
12 December	St Corentin

The lives of the saints

17 January   St Antony of Egypt

Sentence
He will give his angels charge of you to guard you in all your
ways.   (Psalm 91:11 RSV)

Life
St Antony was born in Egypt. His parents were rich and his life
as a young man was comfortable and opulent. In AD 276 his parents died and Antony inherited all their wealth. Shortly after
their death, he heard the story of Jesus telling the rich young
man to sell all that he possessed and give it to the poor. Antony
did not hesitate. He gave away all his possessions and retired
almost immediately to the desert to live a life of solitude.

For more than twenty years Antony lived alone, often not
seeing another human being for six months or more. He was frequently afraid, heard strange noises and was tempted by evil
thoughts, but he strengthened himself with the belief that these
were all the work of Satan who was trying to prevent him from
being a servant of Jesus. Putting on the armour of Christ, he
daily fought these beasts in the desert.

News of this holy man's life and experiences in the desert
spread quickly throughout the Western world and so inspired
young Christians that many forsook their homes and families in
order to emulate Antony's solitary life and find a desert place of
their own.

Gospel
Matthew 3:13–17, 4:1–11; or Matthew 19:16–30

Psalm
91

Collect

Almighty and Most High God, as your servant Antony and the saints of old put their trust in you and found comfort in their solitude, grant that we, through faith, may find the comfort of your presence, not only in our solitude, but in the midst of our busy lives. For it is our busyness and the trappings of this day that are the temptations which separate us from you.

Teach us, Almighty and Most High God, to be quiet and put our trust in you. For the sake of your Son, Jesus Christ our Lord.

Amen.

1 February   *St Brigid*

Sentence

Let your light so shine before men, that they may see your good works and give glory to your Father who is in heaven.

(Matthew 5:16 RSV)

Life

St Brigid was born in Ireland around the year AD 432. Her mother was a slave girl who had been made pregnant by her master. His wife ordered him to sell the slave girl and Brigid's mother was sold to a Druid. Brigid, however, grew up in her mother's faith and was a modest and gentle Christian virgin. Her generosity knew no bounds. She gave away to the poor everything she was given, and much to her father's annoyance even gave away his possessions as well.

When she was eighteen her father tried to arrange a marriage for her, but she refused and left him immediately to become a nun. As she waited at the end of a row of girls waiting to be accepted into the order, the bishop saw a fiery pillar above her head, reaching to the roof. He called her forward, saying, 'Come, holy Brigid, that a veil may be placed over your head before all the others.' Then, it seems, in his confusion, he read from the wrong service and consecrated her bishop by mistake. Afterwards, to justify himself, he explained, 'I have no power. The dignity has already been given her by God.'

Brigid founded many churches, but she is especially known for the convent she established at Kildare. It became known for miles around as 'The City of the Poor' because of her hospitality. There she lit a fire and she and her nuns constantly tended it, keeping it alight as a symbol of faith. The nuns of the convent continued to keep the fire alight for a full thousand years after her death.

Gospel
Luke 10:25–37

Psalm
15

Collect
Almighty God and Father, your servant Brigid served you in all humility and the shining light of her faith burned as a fire in the midst of a pagan land. Grant us, we pray you, such faith and constancy that in your name we may bring the good news of your Son, our Saviour Jesus Christ, to a world that is still in great distress and which continues to call out for help.

Amen.

14 February *St Adwenna*

Sentence
O Lord, our Lord, how majestic is thy name in all the earth!

(Psalm 8:1 RSV)

Life

In the early post-Roman kingdom of Brycheinog in Wales a marriage was arranged between the young princess Marchell and Amlach, a prince from the royal family in Southern Ireland. To bless their union a son was born who was destined to head a dynasty of legendary proportions. His name was Brychan. No fewer than twenty-four saints, both male and female, are reputed to be children of Brychan.

Growing up in the county of Breconshire, the children of this close-knit family were schooled in the Christian faith and eventually set off as missionaries to Cornwall, Devon and Brittany. Dedications to them are found throughout the region, with churches and chapels close enough to each other for the family ties to continue.

Adwenna is remembered in Advent near Camelford in Cornwall. She is attributed as being the patron saint of sweethearts and so it is natural that she has come to share her feast day with St Valentine. Human love, family affection and all that is close to the heart of mankind is epitomized in the hopes and dreams of this Christian family, and in particular in the life of the young virgin Adwenna.

Gospel
John 2:1–12

Psalm
8

Collect
High King of Heaven and father of us all, by our baptism we become part of your family here on earth. In the power of your Holy Spirit knit us together so that in harmony and in peace your Church may go forward and your kingdom spread throughout the world.

In the name of your Son, our Saviour Jesus Christ our Lord.
Amen.

1 March   *St David*

Sentence
He will feed his flock like a shepherd, he will gather the lambs in
his arms.   (Isaiah 40:11 RSV)

Life
David grew up in Wales during the sixth century AD when
Christianity was becoming well established and monasteries and
abbeys were being built. David himself was educated at St Illtyd's
monastery at Llantwit Major, and when he finished his studies
he travelled throughout Wales and south-west England preaching the gospel and founding new communities. He eventually
settled in Mynyw, where he built an abbey and established his
last community and his final home.

David was a gentle, devout man who never tired of teaching
the people and caring for those in need. He spent a great deal
of his time with the sick and homeless, with the orphans and
widows. As he travelled, people flocked around him as sheep
around a shepherd and he was loved and honoured by all who
knew him. Five centuries after his death he was accepted with
much joy as the patron saint of Wales.

Gospel
John 10:1–5, 11–18

Psalm
23

Collect
Dear Lord and Heavenly Father, as your servant David went about on earth gathering the people into the fold of your Church, so imbue the leaders of your Church today with the same spirit of gentleness and humility, that your kingdom may continue to grow and all may be drawn into the presence of your Son, Jesus Christ our Saviour and our Lord.

    Amen.

2 March   *St Chad*

Sentence
I will cry unto God with my voice: even unto God will I cry with my voice, and he shall hearken unto me.   (Psalm 77:1 BCP)

Life
Chad lived in the seventh century AD, and as a child he and his three brothers, Cedd, Cynebil and Caelin, became pupils at the monastery school at Lindisfarne. All four became priests and Chad and Cedd went on to become bishops. When the boys finished their schooling at Lindisfarne, Aidan sent them to Ireland for further study. It was during this period in Ireland that Chad became a priest and in 653 he returned to England to begin his ministry. He came in response to a call from King Penda of Mercia, who wished to arrange for the conversion of his kingdom to Christianity.

    Meanwhile Cedd had been made a bishop in Essex, but in 659 King Ethelwals gave him a piece of land at Lastingham in North Yorkshire on which to build a monastery, of which he was to become abbot. Unfortunately in 664 there was a great plague and Cedd and Cynebil died. Chad travelled to Lastingham and took over the duties of abbot, but his first task was a sad one because he had to bury over thirty of the monks.

    Bishop Tuda of Northumbria also died of the plague and

Wilfred, Abbot of Ripon, was elected to take his place. Wilfred went to Paris for his consecration and enjoyed life in the city so much that he delayed his return. Back in England, King Oswy of Northumberland, growing impatient for Wilfred to return, decided that Chad should be made Bishop in his place. Chad was consecrated at Winchester by two Celtic bishops and one Roman bishop, and returned to take up his duties.

Two years later Wilfred returned and three years after that Chad was told that his consecration was not lawful. Accepting the decision with dignity, Chad retired quietly to Lastingham.

In 669 he was brought out of retirement and appointed as the first Bishop of Mercia at Repton. Very soon afterwards the seat of the diocese was established at Lichfield and Chad became the first Bishop of Lichfield.

Mercia was a large area and Chad tried at first to conduct all his journeys on foot, but Archbishop Theodore, hearing of this, came to Lichfield and presented Chad with the gift of a horse. When Chad demurred, Theodore picked him up and placed him in the saddle. After this Chad accepted the horse!

Chad is remembered in legend for his fear of thunderstorms, which he believed to be sent by God to remind men of the Day of Judgement, and for the story that when King Wulfere came to visit him Wulfere found Chad at prayer and his cell was filled with heavenly light. Wulfere was so impressed that he destroyed the heathen images in his realm and replaced them with monasteries.

Seven days before his death in 672, Chad was visited by a choir of angels and warned that he should prepare to die. Seven days later he was dead. A fellow monk told the historian Bede that he knew a man on the island of Lindisfarne who had seen the soul of Chad's brother Cedd descend from heaven accompanied by angels and carry away Chad's soul to the heavenly kingdom.

Gospel
John 11:1–5, 17–44

Psalm
77

Collect
Almighty God whose servant Chad risked his own life to care for
the brothers at Lastingham who were dying of plague, and who
humbly accepted the decision of the Church and obediently
allowed another to take his place, fill us, we pray, with the same
spirit of discipline and service, that in seeking you in humility we
may find a welcome in your eternal kingdom.
    Amen.

5 March   *St Piran*

Sentence
Let your light so shine before men, that they may see your good
works and give glory to your Father who is in heaven.

(Matthew 5:16 RSV)

Life
Although tradition has St Piran being cast adrift from Ireland
on a millstone and landing on the north Cornwall coast at
Perranporth, it is more likely that he came from Wales. There
was once a medieval chapel of St Piran in Cardiff and in Brittany
he is widely celebrated. Near St Pol de Leon there is a statue of St
Piran in the little church at Trézélidé, while outside in a small
oratory by the roadside there is yet another statue of the saint at
prayer.
    Possibly crossing and recrossing Cornwall several times, his
stopping places still bear his name to this day. Perranporth,
Perranzabuloe, Perranwell, Perrancoombe, Perranuthnoe and

Perranaworthal all bear witness to a saint who was to become adopted by the Cornish as their own. During the Middle Ages the bones, crozier and bell of St Piran were kept at the shrine at Perranzabuloe and attracted many pilgrims. Today the Cornish flag is known as St Piran's cross. The white cross on a black background is said to symbolize the light of the gospel triumphing over the darkness of evil. The mineral wealth of the area gave work to the men of Cornwall and St Piran is especially remembered as the miners' saint.

Gospel
John 9:1–17

Psalm
27:1–7

Collect
Almighty God, Father of us all, with love in his heart and with great courage your servant Piran left his home and family and took the light of the gospel truth into the darkness of the pagan world.

Grant that we, in our turn, may show the love of Christ in all that we do and all that we say.

Give us the courage faithfully to carry the gospel flame entrusted to us to the people of our own generation, that all may see the light and glory of Christ and know for themselves the joy of your kingdom.

Amen.

9 March   *St Constantine*
(*11 March in Scotland*)

Sentence
Fear not, little flock, for it is your Father's good pleasure to give you the kingdom.   (Luke 12:32 RSV)

Life

In the *Vita Petroci* there is a story that, on arriving in Cornwall from Wales, St Petroc protected a stag from a group of huntsmen who returned to report the fact to their master, the Cornish King Constantine. Full of fury, Constantine went to strike the saint with his sword, but was suddenly smitten with paralysis and became unable to move hand or foot. It was St Petroc's prayers that eventually freed him and St Petroc's teaching that converted the King to Christ. In return King Constantine helped St Petroc build his monastery.

King Constantine of Cornwall, one of King Arthur's Knights of the Round Table, held sway over a small kingdom in southern Cornwall during the sixth century AD. A highway near Falmouth linking the area, via the little harbour at Mylor and the now silted port of Tregony, to the northern coast near Padstow is still in parts known as 'My Lord's Road'.

According to Scottish tradition, King Constantine of Cornwall married the daughter of the King of Brittany. When she died, the King refused to be comforted and, handing over the kingdom to his son, he left Cornwall and crossed to Ireland. (In Welsh tradition he went to St David in Wales.) He joined a small monastery and was given the job of carrying grain to the mill. This he did day after day until, taking a rest from his labours, he talked to himself, not knowing that anyone was listening. Shaking his head in disbelief, he said, 'Am I Constantine, King of Cornwall, whose head has so often worn the helmet and his body the breastplate?' 'No!' he replied to himself in despair. The monk who overheard this dialogue reported what he had heard to the abbot, and Constantine was brought into the monastery to become a monk. Later he trained for the priesthood.

After his ordination he travelled with St Columba and then was sent to St Kentigern to establish a church in Galloway. Here he stayed until 576 when, as an elderly abbot visiting the island of Kintyre, he was attacked by four bandits and died a martyr's death.

King, monk and martyr, St Constantine, in true Celtic tradition, has links with Brittany, Cornwall, Ireland, Wales and Scotland and his story is remembered with affection.

Gospel
Mark 10:17–29

Psalm
96

Collect
Eternal High King of Heaven, Almighty God and Father, as your servant Constantine bent the neck of his pride, abandoned his earthly kingdom and gave his life in your service, so may we in quiet humility relinquish the ties of this world, that we may be drawn with cords of love into the kingdom of your Son, our Saviour Jesus Christ.
    Amen.

17 March   *St Patrick*

Sentence
I bind unto myself today
The strong name of the Trinity,
By invocation of the same,
The Three in One and One in Three.

(St Patrick's Breastplate)

Life
St Patrick was the son of a Romano-British deacon named Calpurnius and the grandson of a priest called Potitus. He was born in AD 389 in the village of Bannavem, thought to be in northern England near Carlisle. At the age of sixteen he was captured by raiders and taken as a slave to Ireland. After six years he

managed to escape and was reluctantly given a berth on board a boat carrying hunting dogs to Gaul. In Gaul Patrick entered the monastery at Lerins and in 416 he was ordained deacon at Auxerre by Bishop Amator. He never forgot his time in Ireland and when he was forty-two years old he was given the opportunity to return, being sent to assist Palladius in his mission to stamp out Pelagianism in Ireland. When Palladius died the following year, St Germanus of Auxerre consecrated Patrick as Bishop of Ireland.

By making friends with the High King of Tara, Patrick was able to preach and establish churches without opposition from the authorities. He converted several members of the royal family and in 444 he founded the cathedral church of Armach, which was to become the educational and administrative centre of the Irish Church.

Patrick's allegiance to the Roman Western Church meant that he was often at odds with the Celtic-British Christians, but such was his charisma and genuine devotion to the Irish people that he was held in great affection by all. He was well worthy to be called patron saint of Ireland.

Gospel
Mark 4:35–41

Psalm
46

Collect
Almighty God and Heavenly Father, your servant Patrick conquered his fear and tirelessly preached the good news of your kingdom to an alien race. With courage and in the name of Christ, he made friends with his enemies.

Give us, we pray, both courage and faith and teach us to look upon all those we meet with love and compassion in our hearts,

that through our words and our actions your kingdom may
come on earth and your will be done. We ask this in the name of
Jesus Christ our Lord.

Amen.

20 March   *St Cuthbert*

Sentence
Blessed are the peacemakers, for they shall be called sons of God.

(Matthew 5:9 RSV)

Life
St Cuthbert was born around AD 636 in the Scottish border country near Melrose. While tending sheep in the hill country as a
young teenager, he saw a vision of angels in the sky carrying a
soul to heaven. Leaving the sheep, he went straight to the
monastery at Melrose, where they told him that the great St
Aidan had just died. Cuthbert immediately offered himself for
the religious life, vowing to continue Aidan's work in spreading
the gospel throughout Northumbria.

Cuthbert became Prior of Melrose and then, in 664, the year
of the Synod at Whitby, he travelled to Lindisfarne. His friend
Eata became Abbot and Cuthbert was made Prior.

At the Synod of Whitby the decision had been made that the
Celtic Church would come into line with the authoritarian disciplines of the Roman Church. Cuthbert was a peace-loving man
who believed that it was quite possible for the two disciplines to
live in harmony, and he conducted the life of the monks at
Lindisfarne accordingly. The Roman tonsure and the Roman date
of Easter were both adopted and Cuthbert improved the discipline of the monastery, but in all else, Lindisfarne remained
distinctly Celtic in character.

Holding the two disciplines in juxtaposition and cajoling,
encouraging and mediating between those monks who were not

prepared to compromise took its toll on Cuthbert's health and in the end he retired. He died on Lindisfarne and in 995 his body was taken to Durham Cathedral.

Gospel
Matthew 5:1–12

Psalm
133 or 91

Collect
Almighty God by whose grace St Cuthbert walked the path of peace and created in Lindisfarne a place of sanctuary for monks, pilgrims and people alike, grant that we too, in all humility, may learn to live together in unity so that your peace may spread throughout the world and the whole earth become the sanctuary of our Lord and Saviour Jesus Christ.
    Amen.

27 April   *St Enoder (also known as Tenenan, Tinidor and Ternoc)*

Sentence
My soul hath a desire and longing to enter into the courts of the Lord: my heart and my flesh rejoice in the living God.

(Psalm 84:2 BCP)

Life
As a young man, newly ordained, St Carantoc left his native Wales and travelled to Ireland, where he was to stay for many years helping a now elderly St Patrick build up the Church in Ireland. Carantoc established churches and monasteries and many a noble family sent their children to him for schooling. A child named Enoder, the son of an Irish prince, studied with him and when he had completed his studies Enoder was sent by his

parents to London, to the King's court, where the only daughter of the Count of Arondel fell in love with him. Enoder was a very handsome young man but had set his heart on becoming a monk, and he was desperately afraid that the Count of Arondel and his father would make marriage arrangements. To avoid the match, Enoder prayed earnestly that he might become so ugly that none would marry him. His prayer was heard and he became a leper. The marriage plans were aborted and Enoder thankfully returned to Ireland, planning to offer himself to Carantoc as an oblate.

Carantoc, having been warned by God of Enoder's condition, was waiting for him. He welcomed him gladly and gave him a meal and then compelled him to take a bath. Enoder was embarrassed and afraid, but Carantoc was insistent. When Enoder entered the bath Carantoc touched his skin and he was healed. Enoder was upset to be returned to his handsome self, because he knew that his looks not only made him proud but also made him the object of desire. He was angry with his old teacher, but Carantoc just shrugged and said, 'Now you don't stink!'

From this moment onwards Enoder remained with Carantoc as his disciple. They left Ireland in around 520 accompanied by two other disciples, both of whom were named Columb, and travelled back to Wales and then on to Somerset and Cornwall. On arrival in Cornwall they built an oratory on the north coast and from this base Carantoc sent his young disciples out to found their own parishes. Enoder established his first church near a spring and a settlement not far from the coast, while the two Columbs founded their churches nearby. It is believed that one of the Columbs was martyred in Cornwall and that after a few years the others continued their travels and went to Brittany, accompanied by Senan, Quenan and several others.

Enoder founded three churches in Leon, at Plou-bennec, Les-quelen and Landerneau, and then as years went by he decided to take himself into retreat and built a little cell at a place now called Lan-Tinidor, not far from the tidal river of Ylorna. How long he stayed there we do not know, but as an elderly man he succeeded St Goulben as Bishop of the see of St Pol de Leon.

The first thing he did when he became bishop was to found a church in honour of St Carantoc. This is now the parish church of Carantec in Leon. In humility Bishop Enoder had himself represented as a little disciple at the feet of his kind master. Ever since, statues of St Carantoc have been accompanied by a little Enoder.

Gospel
Luke 17:11–19

Psalm
84

Collect
Almighty God and Heavenly Father, as your servant Enoder recognized the great influence in his life of his teacher Carantoc and never ceased to give thanks for his education, so may we be thankful for all those men and women who have helped to mould us and lead us in the way of our Lord and Saviour Jesus Christ.
    Amen.

28 April   *St Guenole*

Sentence
The fear of the Lord is the beginning of wisdom; a good understanding have all those who practise it.   (Psalm 111:10 RSV)

Life
St Guenole was born in Brittany during the fifth century AD to an emigrant Cornish family. He proved to be such an intelligent,

questioning child that his father took him to St Budoc and asked him if he would take Guenole as his student. Budoc knew Cornwall well and was sympathetic to the family. He allowed Guenole to stay and took a personal interest in his upbringing.

As he grew up within the monastery Guenole gained a reputation for his miraculous works. While he was still a young man he went to Budoc and begged to be allowed to leave the monastery and lead a missionary party to Ireland. Budoc, however, did not consider that Guenole was mature enough for such a venture and, although Guenole continued to beg, Budoc stood firm.

Eventually Guenole was given permission to choose twelve disciples and to go and establish a monastery in Brittany. Disappointed that he was not being asked to travel the seas further afield, Guenole nevertheless set off to find a suitable site.

After an abortive attempt at establishing an island site, Guenole and his disciples finally settled in a sheltered valley situation and began to build. The great monastery of Landevennec still flourishes to this day.

Guenole never left this site. He remained as a much loved abbot and died in this beautiful spot. His dream of travelling to Ireland never became a reality, but under his direction his monks are known to have travelled to Cornwall and Wales. Perhaps in time we will discover that they did indeed succeed in reaching the Ireland of Guenole's dream.

Gospel
John 21:1–23

Psalm
111

Collect
Almighty God, by whose grace the blessed St Guenole became a burning and shining light in your Church, kindle in us the same

spirit of discipline and love, that we may ever walk before you as children of light; through Jesus Christ our Lord.

Amen.

1 May   St Brioc

Sentence

My soul magnifies the Lord, and my spirit rejoices in God my Saviour.

(Luke 1:46 RSV)

Life

St Brioc was born in Cardiganshire during the sixth century AD. His father, Cerpus, was a wealthy nobleman from a Roman family and he and his household continued to worship the Roman and Celtic gods.

One night his wife Eldruda received a vision of an angel who told her that she had been chosen by God to give birth to a special child, 'a son, dear to God and of great merit'. The angel told her to persuade her husband to give up his idolatrous ways and prepare for the coming child. When he heard what his wife had to say, Cerpus was scornful and dismissive. The angel then appeared to him and began to scourge him for his disobedience and Cerpus very quickly changed his mind and destroyed his gods.

When the little boy was born it quickly became obvious that he was indeed special. He was intelligent and quick to learn and eventually his parents sent him to St Germanus in Paris to advance his learning.

In Paris Brioc learnt his lessons well and the monks were amazed at his generosity and strength of faith. Even as a child he is reputed to have performed many miracles. When, as a young man, he was ordained by Germanus, that great churchman was amazed to see a pillar of fire reaching to the roof of the church, hovering over the head of young Brioc.

At the age of twenty-five Brioc also experienced a vision of an angel who told him to return to Wales and convert his parents. On his return he did indeed convert his parents and many of the people, who were amazed by his power to heal and by his teaching. He set about establishing a monastery and many churches, and became greatly revered in his home country.

After a while he decided to travel once more and, leaving Wales, he crossed Cornwall and journeyed to Brittany. Here too he built a monastery, possibly at Tréguier, and here he proposed to settle. But a deputation from Cardigan came to him in great urgency, telling him of disasters at home, and Brioc returned once more to Wales.

On his return the people begged him to stay, but once the problems were over Brioc set off yet again to Brittany. Landing on a different part of the coast, he and his party were intercepted by some men serving Count Rigual and were taken to the Count's dwelling. Rigual was ill, tormented by agonizing pains, but when Brioc came into his presence the pains abated and he was restored to health. In gratitude Rigual gave Brioc a beautiful portion of land and Brioc and his monks began to build another monastery, this time at the present Saint-Brieuc.

The new monastery became a model for all others in the area and in great contentment Brioc remained here until he died.

Gospel
Luke 1:26–38

Psalm
24

Collect
Almighty God, by whose grace St Brioc lived among us in purity and in faith, grant us the grace to live our lives in such a way that all may see in us the love of your Son, our Saviour Jesus

Christ, at work in the world.
   Amen.

5 May   *St Gwinear*

Sentence
The water that I shall give him will become in him a spring of
water welling up to eternal life.   (John 4:14 RSV)

Life
St Gwinear's origins are obscured by legend and it is difficult to
determine whether he came from Wales or Ireland. He is com-
memorated in both Cornwall and Brittany and the parishes dedicated to him are very close to those dedicated to St Meriadoc.
This has given rise to the theory that Gwinear and Meriadoc
were Welsh missionaries who travelled together and who, after
converting the Cornish and establishing churches there, both
then travelled on to Brittany.
   The legends of St Gwinear in both Cornwall and Brittany,
however, tell us that he was Irish. St Patrick had called together a
gathering of chieftains in southern Ireland and the young man
Gwinear was the only one to honour the saint and offer him a
seat. His father Clito, who wanted no change from the worship
of the ancient gods, banished Gwinear and many of his friends.
The young men sailed to Brittany and while out hunting one
day, Gwinear struck his spear in the ground and a fountain
miraculously sprang up. As he washed in the water and considered the miracle, he was moved to devote himself entirely to the
Lord's service and spent many years as a hermit and then as
abbot of a small monastery in Brittany.
   Warned by an angel in a dream that it was time to return to
his native land, Gwinear set sail once more. On his return he
found Ireland now a Christian country and his father Clito dead.
The people begged Gwinear to stay and take the throne, but he

was determined to continue his work for the Lord. After encouraging many to join him, Gwinear, his sister Piala (or Phillack), a large party of would-be missionaries and seven bishops set sail for Cornwall. They arrived at Hayle and travelled inland. At their first camp there was no fresh water, so Gwinear struck the ground with his staff and a fountain sprang up from which the young men quenched their thirst.

Unknown to the missionaries, a message had been relayed to King Tudor (or Theodoric) of Cornwall that his land had been invaded by the Irish. He and his soldiers sped to the scene on horseback and soon surrounded the Christians. Without hesitation they began to attack. Gwinear and a small band of men were exploring further up the valley and survived this first massacre, but Tudor soon caught up with them and with his own sword cut off Gwinear's head.

According to legend, Gwinear knelt down and picked up his head, carrying it to a secluded, peaceful place where he planted his staff in the ground and lay down to die. In Brittany there is an identical story which tells us that Gwinear died in the same manner at Pluvigner.

Gospel
John 4:1–42

Psalm
63

Collect
Almighty God and Heavenly Father, as your servant Gwinear was refreshed by your gift of living water and led by your Spirit to lead a life of discipleship and martyrdom, so inspire us with these wondrous gifts that we too may be filled with confidence and joy, and may serve you in humility all our days.

Amen.

16 May   *St Carantoc*
(26 May in Wales)

Sentence
All things are possible with God.   (Mark 10:27 RSV)

Life
Carantoc was the son of Ceretic, the legendary founder of the
principality of Cardigan, and was able to trace his ancestry back
to Anna, the cousin of Mary, the mother of Jesus. He was of
kingly birth and very wealthy, but he forsook both position and
wealth and went to live as a hermit in a cave at Edilu.

Later, as a young priest, he was to leave Wales and travel to
Ireland, where he offered his services to an elderly and ailing St
Patrick and helped him with his task of evangelizing the Irish.

In Ireland, legend tells us, Carantoc began to build a
monastery and was in need of timber. Nearby a tyrant king
named Dulcemius owned forests and one large tree in particular.
Carantoc wanted this tree to use for the foundation of his building and he went to the king to beg permission to use it. The king
replied that if he could fell the tree by prayer alone, it could be
his. Carantoc replied, 'Nothing is impossible to God,' and he
knelt to pray. His prayer finished, Carantoc stood up and the tree
fell to the ground.

Back in Wales, the disciples he had left behind had built a
flourishing monastery around his cave at Edilu, which Carantoc
visited again, this time on his way to Somerset accompanied by
his disciple Tenenan (also known as Tinidor or Enoder).

In Somerset we are told that Carantoc helped King Arthur by
subduing a dragon and then he continued on his travels, crossing
Cornwall and eventually settling in Brittany.

Legend tells us that on his journeys he was accompanied at
all times by two doves (*columba* means 'dove' in Latin), or more
probably by two disciples both bearing the Irish name of
Columb. Apparently he was directed in his travels by casting

his altar stone into the sea and waiting to see where it came ashore.

Interestingly, in Cornwall the parish of Crantock is close to two parishes dedicated to St Columb, and nearby is the parish of St Enoder. In Brittany the parish of Carantec is close to Plougoulm (Parish of Columb) and there are many dedications in the area to Tenenan and Tinidor.

Gospel
Matthew 17

Psalm
29

Collect
Almighty God and Heavenly Father, as your servant Carantoc scorned riches and high position to become a servant of the Church, grant that through faith we too may become humble in spirit, putting away all pride and stubbornness, and being content to play our part quietly in the building of your kingdom here on earth, in the name of your Son, our Lord and Saviour Jesus Christ.

Amen.

4 June   *St Petroc*

Sentence
The steadfast love of the Lord is from everlasting to everlasting.

(Psalm 103:17 RSV)

Life
St Petroc is said to have been the son of a Welsh chieftain, born in the sixth century AD. As a young man, he was first educated in a monastery in south Wales and then travelled with a group of

friends to study in Ireland. He stayed in Ireland for twenty years and then, still in the company of his group of friends, he set sail for Cornwall, landing in the Camel Estuary. On the spot where he landed Petroc, with the help of King Constantine of Cornwall, established a monastic centre which later became known as Petroc-stow or Padstow.

Like most of his Celtic holy men, Petroc held to a very strict rule and each day from cockcrow to dawn he would be found standing up to his neck in the cold sea, reciting psalms. His dedication drew many to him and the little community flourished. Eventually, feeling confident that the monks could manage for a while without him, Petroc set out on a pilgrimage of a lifetime. He visited Rome and then Jerusalem, and finally went on to India. Legend tells us that one day, as he stood by the seashore, a huge silver bowl appeared. Taking off his cloak and putting his staff down on the beach, Petroc stepped into the bowl and was taken by the wind to a small island where he lived for seven years, surviving on a single fish a day. At the end of seven years the bowl reappeared and Petroc returned to the shore, finding his cloak and staff safely lying where he had put them, guarded by a large wolf.

Petroc returned to Cornwall and built himself a small chapel and hermitage further inland from Padstow at Little Petherick. In due course, he travelled even further inland, to a stretch of moorland where he built himself a small beehive hut. Unable even there to escape the students who continued to want to be with him, Petroc established his last and greatest community at Bodmin.

Petroc died on a visit to Padstow and was buried there, but the monks of Padstow eventually moved to Bodmin and took his bones with them. The ancient casket that held his bones can now be seen in St Petroc's Church, Bodmin.

Gospel
Matthew 6:19–34

Psalm
103

Collect
Almighty God, who sent your servant Petroc to build up your
Church in Cornwall, grant that we, trusting in you in all things,
may labour faithfully to build on the same foundation, even
Jesus Christ, your Son, our Lord.
    Amen.

7 June   *St Meriadoc*

Sentence
The Lord will fulfil his purpose for me; thy steadfast love, O Lord,
endures for ever.   (Psalm 138:8 RSV)

Life
St Meriadoc, as his name suggests, was probably born in Wales
and travelled south accompanied by Gwinear. Their parishes lie
side by side in both Cornwall and southern Brittany but, while
Gwinear died a martyr's death, Meriadoc eventually became
Bishop of Vannes.

    The Cornish miracle play *Beunans Meriasek* tells of the saint's
exploits in both Cornwall and Brittany, but the stories of his life
which were later written in Brittany make no mention of either
Wales or Cornwall.

    According to Breton tradition, Meriadoc was of royal birth
and was educated at the king's court. When his time at court was
over he was determined to turn his back on positions of wealth
and enter the Church. His father tried to dissuade him, but when
he realized that Meriadoc was serious he bought for his son the

richest benefices in the area. Meriadoc was ordained, but after saying his first Mass he resolved to retire to a desert place where his family's wealth and position could not corrupt him.

He finally obtained his bishop's permission and he sold the benefices, giving the money to the poor, and found himself a solitary place in the viscounty of Rohan. He lived simply and spent his time in prayer. His saintliness attracted people from all over Brittany and they flocked to visit him.

When the Bishop of Vannes died the clergy and people assembled to elect a new bishop and unanimously agreed on Meriadoc. A deputation was sent to fetch him to the city and a reluctant Meriadoc left the solitude he so loved and became Bishop of Vannes. He fulfilled his duties with compassion and humility and was loved by all. When he died his body was buried in his cathedral.

Gospel
Matthew 6:1–15

Psalm
138

Collect
O God, who didst deliver blessed Meriadoc thy confessor and pontiff from this famine-stricken world, and bring him, through a life of voluntary poverty, to the land of everlasting brightness: grant, we beseech thee, that at his intercessions the chains of our iniquity may be broken.

Amen.

(Collect found in the Vannes 'Proper' of 1630)

9 June   *St Columba*

Sentence
See that you are at peace among yourselves, my children, and
love one another.   (St Columba)

Life
St Columba (the dove of God) was born in December of AD 520
in Donegal, Ireland. He attended a number of monastic schools
and was later ordained into the priesthood. Until the age of
about forty he travelled throughout Ireland setting up monastic
centres of learning, including those at Kells and Derry.

   In 561 Columba was accused of copying a prayer book
belonging to St Finnian without permission. He was reluctant to
give up the copy that had taken so long in writing and Finnian
was so enraged that a battle ensued.

   Forced to leave his beloved Ireland, Columba and twelve
companions set sail in a wicker-and-hide currach (coracle) and
landed eventually on the tiny island of Iona. When he finally
died before the altar of his island church, Columba's face was
radiant with joy and his hand was outstretched in blessing.

Gospel
Matthew 18:12–22

Psalm
42

Collect
High King of Heaven, Almighty Father of us all, as your servant
Columba established a community built on love and trust which
still spreads its light and influence throughout the world, so
grant that in all humility we may be your hands and your voices
here on earth, working for ever and building a community of
faith in the name of your Son, our Saviour Jesus Christ.
   Amen.

15 June   *St Non*

Sentence
Search me, O God, and know my heart! Try me and know my
thoughts!   (Psalm 139:23 RSV)

Life
St Non was the mother of St David. She was from a noble family
and became a student at the monastery at Ty Gwyn in Wales.
The monastery was visited by a young king of Cardigan named
Sant, who had just renounced his throne in order to become a
monk. Sant and Non fell in love and for the short period of
Sant's visit they managed to keep their relationship a secret.
When Sant left, Non discovered she was pregnant. Although she
was able to hide the fact for several months, she was eventually
discovered and was banished in disgrace from the monastery.

Unable to return home, she took shelter in a mountain hut
near the standing stones beyond Bryn Y Garn and finally gave
birth to a stillborn baby boy during a violent thunderstorm.

Present at the birth was St Ailbe, who quickly plunged the
child into the icy waters at a nearby pool, causing the baby to
gasp and cry aloud. After baptizing the baby in a spring, Ailbe
agreed to care for him and Non travelled to Cornwall, where she
founded the church of Altarnon. The adjacent parish is known as
Davidstow and it is thought that David later visited his mother,
staying long enough to establish a church which later became
dedicated to him.

Gospel
John 12:1–8

Psalm
139:1–13

Collect
Almighty God, whose servant Non suffered pain and great loss and yet still remained faithful and true, grant us such grace that as we are tried and tempted by the world around us we too will continue to keep steady the flame of faith, until the whole world is ablaze with your glory.
    Amen.

28 July   *St Samson*

Sentence
Let the words of my mouth and the meditation of my heart be acceptable in thy sight, O Lord, my rock and my redeemer.

(Psalm 19:14 RSV)

Life
Samson was born in south-west Wales around AD 490. He was taken as a youth to be a student of the great teacher Illtyd at Llantwit Major and was ordained by Bishop Dubricius. He became abbot of a monastery at Caldy Island off the Pembrokeshire coast and from there he frequently visited Ireland. On one visit he purchased what the writer of his *Life* calls a chariot, but which was probably a small donkey cart or wheelbarrow.

For a short period he withdrew to a hermitage on the banks of the Severn. When he returned to Llantwit Major he was elected bishop, but it was revealed to him that he should give up his monastic existence and become a *peregrinus*, or travelling holy man, leaving his native land to journey overseas.

Samson's method of travelling was unique. When he was travelling overland he was able to fold his coracle and sail and place them in his Irish 'chariot', and horses were hired to draw it along the road. On reaching the sea once more, the coracle was put back together and the chariot was lifted into it for the journey over the water. The chariot also carried all Samson's holy books, food and tools.

Travelling south from Wales, Samson crossed Cornwall from Padstow to Fowey, on what is now known as Saint's Way, and from there he set sail for Brittany. As he travelled, Samson claimed many people for Christ and took pride in scratching the sign of a cross on many a pagan standing stone.

In Brittany he founded a number of churches and monasteries, even travelling to Paris, where he was in contact with Childebert, King of Paris. His most famous monastery is at Dol.

Psalm
Luke 10:1–9

Psalm
19

Collect
Almighty God, by whose grace blessed Samson journeyed through the Western lands to preach the gospel of your Son, grant that we may always be ready to proclaim your love in every place and be faithful to your holy name. We make our prayer through Jesus Christ our Lord.

Amen.

31 August   *St Aidan*

Sentence
All the ends of the earth have seen the salvation of our God.

(Psalm 98:3 RSV)

Life
In AD 633 King Oswald of Northumbria attempted to convert his people to Christianity. Like many young noblemen, Oswald had

been educated at Iona and so it was to Iona and the Celtic Church that King Oswald turned for help in finding a missionary for his people. The monk Corman was the first to be sent, but he returned with the report that the people of Northumbria were an 'obstinate, barbarous people'.

The monk Aidan, who was present when Corman reported to the abbot, replied, 'Brother, it seems to me that you were too severe on your ignorant hearers. You should have followed the practice of the Apostles, and begun by giving them the milk of simpler teaching, and gradually nourished them with the word of God until they were capable of greater perfection and able to follow the loftier precepts of Christ' (from Bede's *A History of the English Church and People*). Recognizing the wisdom of Aidan's words, the community consecrated him as bishop and in 635 Aidan left Iona with twelve companions and travelled to Northumbria.

Aidan established a monastery on Holy Island, or Lindisfarne as it is also known, off the Northumbrian coast. The island was cut off twice a day by the tide, but looked directly across to the mainland and Oswald's castle at Bamburgh. Aidan the monk and Oswald the king supported each other in their work and Oswald often accompanied Aidan on his missionary journeys. Lindisfarne became the cradle of Christianity in north-east England and a great centre of learning and prayer.

When Oswald died, Aidan continued to travel alone, always by foot and always stopping to speak to both rich and poor. He baptized and befriended countless people, and was loved by all. By the time he died in 651 the fire of Christianity was burning brightly in Northumbria.

Gospel
Luke 10:25–37

Psalm
98

Collect
Almighty God and Heavenly Father, your servant Aidan drew
men and women into your family the Church with cords of compassion. In his life the love of your Son shone in the world as a
burning light. Grant us, O Lord, the grace to keep the light burning and to work in the world to your praise and glory.
      Amen.

16 September   *St Ninian*

Sentence
I will sing to the Lord as long as I live; I will sing praise to my
God while I have being.   (Psalm 104:33 RSV)

Life
St Ninian was born on the northern shores of the Solway Firth
around AD 360. His father was a converted chieftain of the
Cumbrian Britons who wanted his son to be a soldier. Ninian,
however, had other ideas and from a very early age was determined to dedicate his life to God. The great Celtic centres of
learning were not yet established and, determined to receive a
Christian education, the young Ninian travelled to Rome, where
he studied for many years. He was ordained priest and finally, in
394, he was consecrated bishop by Pope Siricus in order to
return home to convert his native Scotland.
      On his journey home he visited St Martin at Tours and was
greatly impressed by this charismatic teacher. When he finally
returned to the Solway Firth, he built his first church at
Whithorn, a small square building of local stone covered with
white mortar, which became known as the *Candida Casa*, or
White House. Ninian dedicated the church to his friend Martin of

Tours, who died in 397, the year that the building was completed.

From the *Candida Casa*, Ninian and his monks set out to convert the neighbouring Britons and the Picts of the former Roman province of Valentia. They were remarkably successful and Ninian, with his tall, soldierly build and his family connections, was able to talk on equal terms with the warlike tribal chieftains. The *Candida Casa* became a centre of Christian learning for many centuries after Ninian's death in 432.

Like his friend and hero St Martin, Ninian found himself a cave where he could retreat for days on end to meditate and pray. During the Middle Ages this cave became a focal point for many pilgrimages, and crosses have been carved in the cliff walls by the numerous devotees who made the journey.

Gospel
Mark 6:45–56

Psalm
148

Collect
High King of Heaven and Lord of All, your servant Ninian worked with courage and initiative to take the good news of your kingdom to the people of Scotland. Give to your Church that same courage to fight against evil and to act fearlessly in the name of your Son, our Lord and Saviour Jesus Christ.

Amen.

3 October   *St Kea*

Sentence
O be joyful in the Lord, all ye lands : serve the Lord with gladness, and come before his presence with a song. (Psalm 100:1 BCP)

Life

St Kea is a romantic figure linked in legend to the story of Arthur. It is quite likely that he was Sir Kay, Arthur's steward.

St Kea was born in Wales at the end of the fifth century AD. Like all the Celtic saints he travelled about, settling for a while in Glastonbury, where he made friends with the historian Gildas and built his own hermitage at Leigh, on the sloping hills surrounding the shallow lakes. Then he journeyed on through Devon and Cornwall and over to Brittany. In Brittany he is known as St Quary and he founded a monastery at Cleder.

Many of the Arthur stories portray Kay as an impetuous young man ready to argue and often saying the wrong thing at the wrong time. But it is as a peacemaker that St Kea is best remembered. With the days of his unruly youth behind him, Kea eventually became a responsible abbot. When the continual conflict between Arthur and his nephew Mordred threatened to disturb the newly found period of peace after the battle of Mount Baden, Kea returned from Brittany to try and bring about peace between the two enemies. He did not succeed, but stayed with Arthur as he struggled to hold the old kingdom together. He apparently managed to persuade Guinevere to enter a nunnery, and later returned to his monastery in Brittany, where it is believed he died.

Gospel
Luke 19:11–27

Psalm
99 and 100

Collect
High King of Heaven, Almighty God and Father, your servant Kea remained faithful to his friends and did not despise their wealth and position in life. Instead he used his skills to assist

them to become responsible and wise rulers. Give to us your servants the ability to show your love in the world, in our homes and in our places of work, so that your kingdom may come on earth and your will be done.

Amen.

10 October *St Paul Aurelian*

Sentence
If you abide in me, and my words abide in you, ask whatever you will, and it shall be done for you.   (John 15:7 RSV)

Life
Paul was born around AD 495 in south Wales. Descended from Roman nobility, his family name of Aurelian is remembered to this day. He was educated by Illtyd at Llantwit Major and his companions included David, Gildas and Samson. After he was ordained he lived as a hermit in Llandovery, spending many years in isolation in his 'desert place'. Gradually, however, his piety attracted admirers. As increasing numbers of disciples joined him, he founded a monastery at Llanddensant, on moorland below the Black Mountain.

Eventually Paul took twelve of his students and left his native Wales. They travelled to the court of King Mark in Cornwall and on from there to the home of Paul's sister Sitofolla, who lived near Newlyn in Mount's Bay. The level of the sea was lower then than it is now, and large tracts of forest stretched out on land that is now covered by sea. By the shores of Gwavas Lake in the middle of the forest, Paul helped his sister build a small chapel. Many years later, when the sea encroached, the chapel was abandoned and rebuilt on top of the nearby hill where the village and church of Paul can be found today.

Paul and his companions travelled on to Brittany, where Paul was given the island of Batz on which to build a monastery. It

was not long, however, before the local people begged him to
become their bishop. He was consecrated at Leon, the town
which now bears the name of St Pol de Leon and where Paul's
bell is a treasured relic. *The Life of St Pol* was written in 884.

Gospel
John 2:1–11

Psalm
1

Collect
Almighty God and Heavenly Father, through your servant Paul
you have wrought great works and in his words and deeds your
Son Jesus Christ was seen on earth once more. Cleanse our souls
so that we too may follow in the footsteps of our Lord, and in us
others may see a little of the wonderful light of your love.
    Amen.

17 October   *St Levan (also known as Selevan)*

Sentence
Thy testimonies, O Lord, are very sure : holiness becometh thine
house for ever.   (Psalm 93:6)

Life
St Levan lived during the fifth century AD and appears to have
been a member of a small, Cornish noble family. As it is known
that both his father and grandfather were Christians, this would
date his family roots back to the time of St Martin at least.
    St Levan established his cell near a well beside a small stream
which tumbles down the West Penwith cliffs. His brother St Just
made his home further round the coast, and his sister Silwen
also lived nearby. St Levan appears to have been very fond of

fishing and once when his sister and two small children visited him, he cooked them two of the chad he had just caught. The children ate quickly and one of them choked on the bones. The child came to no harm, but for many centuries the St Levan fishermen called the chad 'chuck cheeld', or choke child. In the little church that was built in the saint's name there are two fish carved on a bench end.

Outside the church on the south side there is a giant boulder which has been dramatically split in two. Legend has it that St Levan struck the boulder with his staff and caused it to crack. He then prophesied that if the crack ever widened to be large enough for a pack horse carrying panniers to ride between the stones, the end of the world would come.

In nearby St Just there is an ancient tombstone with a Latin inscription, and it is known that the relics of Levan's brother St Just were housed there up to the fifteenth century and possibly beyond. Of his sister Silwen there is no lasting memorial.

Gospel
Matthew 20:1–19

Psalm
93

Collect
High King of Heaven, Eternal Lord God, your servant St Levan led a life of simplicity and peace, content only to walk continually in your presence. Through his constant and abiding faith many people down the ages have been drawn with cords of love into your kingdom. Grant that we, living our everyday lives, may find the same contentment so that others may see in us the loving grace of your Son, our Saviour Jesus Christ.
Amen.

27 October   *St Ia*
(originally 3 February; 18 September in Brittany)

Sentence
O sing to the Lord a new song; sing to the Lord, all the earth!

(Psalm 96:1 RSV)

Life
By tradition Ia (Hya) was an Irish princess who was converted to
Christianity by St Patrick and who longed to join the young
monks on their missionary journeys. When Gwinear and his
companions left Ireland to sail for Cornwall, Ia hurried to the
shore determined to go with them. Finding she was too late, she
knelt down on the beach in great grief and prayed. As she did so
she saw a little leaf floating on the water. She prodded it and
suddenly, as she touched it, it began to grow until it became as
large as a small boat. Eagerly stepping aboard, Ia hurriedly set
sail to catch the others. A wind from God caught her sail and she
sped across the Channel, arriving at the coast of Cornwall ahead
of Gwinear and a little further to the west. As a result she
avoided the massacre which Gwinear and his followers were
subject to and was even able to use her charms to persuade a
Cornish warlord called Dinan to build a small chapel for her at
Pendinis, and it is here that the town of St Ives now stands.

Legend aside, it is likely that Ia did indeed come from Ireland
and travelled on her missionary journeys with Euny, Elwin and
possibly Anta. After establishing parishes on the coast of
Cornwall, they travelled inland to the Camborne, Helston area
and then set sail for Brittany. Dedications to them can be found
all along this route.

Gospel
Matthew 15:22–33

Psalm
96

Collect
King of the Universe, Spirit of the Living God, with a wind from heaven you sped your servant St Ia on her way so that she might answer your call to labour for your kingdom. May the mighty power of your spirit work in our lives, that we may respond to your word with love in our hearts and sing to your praise with great joy.
    Amen.

6 November   *St Illtyd*

Sentence
You shall love the Lord your God with all your heart, and with all your soul, and with all your mind.   (Matthew 22:37 RSV)

Life
St Illtyd lived between AD 450 and 535. It is thought that he was born in Brittany and that he became a disciple of St Germanus of Auxerre at the monastery founded by Cassian at Marseilles. He is said to have come to England in about 470.

    Other, nonhistorical traditions claim that he was cousin to King Arthur and that he served him as a knight. It is said that he was converted to Christianity after an earthquake killed many of his companions on a hunting expedition.

    Illtyd is known to have travelled around Brittany, Cornwall and Wales establishing monasteries and churches. It is, however, the monastery at Llantwit Major in the Vale of Glamorgan that is his most well known foundation. Many young men came to study there and it became famous as a centre of learning. St Illtyd himself was a prodigious scholar, as the writer of St Samson's *Life* tells us: 'Of all the Britons, he [St Illtyd] was the most learned in all the scriptures, and in those of philosophy of every kind, specifically of geometry and of rhetoric, grammar and arithmetic, and all of the theories of philosophy.'

David, Samson, Gildas (the first British historian) and Paul Aurelian were all his students. According to legend, Illtyd enlisted their help to mark out a new boundary to the monastery lands. When the tide was out, Illtyd walked down the sands and marked a furrow with his staff along the low-water mark, then he and his students stood along the furrow and forbade the sea to pass. Needless to say, the sea obeyed!

Illtyd was a conscientious and brilliant teacher, but sometimes he needed to withdraw and be quiet for a while. His favourite retreat was an oratory at Oxwith, but he is also known to have spent time at St Michael's Mount in Cornwall and in Brittany.

Gospel
Matthew 22:34–46

Psalm
119:33–48

Collect
Almighty God and Heavenly Father, you gave to your servant Illtyd the gifts of wisdom and understanding, and using these talents he spread the gospel of your Son Jesus Christ our Saviour to all he met. Grant that we, in all humility, may not be ashamed to use the gifts you have given us, so that we may join the ranks of your followers and that through us your kingdom may come at last.

Amen.

8 November   *St Cuby (also spelt Cybi)*

Sentence
You who fear the Lord, trust in the Lord!   (Psalm 115:11 RSV)

Life
Cuby was the son of a Cornish military leader and local king named Solomon or Selevan. His mother was Gwen, sister of Non, the mother of David. Cuby was brought up and went to school in Cornwall, where he lived until he was twenty-seven years of age. Then he went on a pilgrimage to Jerusalem that took him away for three years. On his return he was ordained and set about establishing his first churches, probably at Duloe and Tregony. In both instances the churches nearby are dedicated to his aunt Non, and near Duloe there are dedications to his mother and father.

We are not sure what happened to Selevan. If he is the same Selevan to be found in West Cornwall we must surmise that he retired to live the life of a holy man or hermit. If he is not the same person then he probably died while Cuby was still a young man, for the local people were determined that Cuby should succeed him as their king. Cuby, however, had other ideas and with ten disciples he left Cornwall for good.

He travelled first to Wales, where he founded two churches in Monmouthshire, at Llangibby and Llandauer Guir. He and his disciples did not stay long in Wales and once the churches were established they set sail for Ireland.

Cuby went first to the island of Aran Mor to meet up with St Enda, who he had first met on his pilgrimage to Jerusalem. Cuby and his disciples stayed on the island for four years, but it was not a happy time. Cuby's uncle Cyngar was travelling with them and was now a very old man and needed constant nursing. Cuby bought a cow to provide the old man with milk, but its calf got out of the pen and wandered into the vegetable garden of Fintan, one of Enda's priests. Fintan was furious and a feud was started, not helped by Cuby's Cornish followers who continued to aggravate the enraged priest.

In the end, when Cyngar died Cuby and his disciples moved again, hoping to find a more peaceful place to continue their ministry, but it was not to be in Ireland. Every time they settled somewhere Fintan would find them and stir up the locals against them. In the end they left Ireland for good and returned to Wales, this time to Anglesey.

In Anglesey Cuby met Maelgwn, King of Gwynedd, and managed to acquire rights to the whole of the promontory on the north-west of the island. Eventually he persuaded Maelgwn to give him the fortress at its very tip. The fortress was an old Roman castle and it was within the battlements that Cuby built his monastery. The headland became known as Caer Gybi and there Cuby settled and established a religious foundation that became renowned for its teaching and the piety of its monks.

Gospel
Luke 8:4–15

Psalm
122

Collect
Almighty God, whose servant Cuby travelled afar and established a great monastery, famous as a seat of learning, guide us in our pilgrim path and guard us from all adversity so that we too may fulfil our calling and play our part in building your kingdom here on earth. In the name of your Son, our Saviour Jesus Christ.

Amen.

11 November *St Martin*

Sentence
Come, O blessed of my Father, inherit the kingdom prepared for
you from the foundation of the world. (Matthew 25:34 RSV)

Life
St Martin was born in Hungary and enlisted in the Roman army
as an officer. In the winter of AD 337 when the army was serving
in Amiens in France, a semi-naked beggar approached him one
day, shivering with cold. Much to the amusement of his fellow
officers, Martin sliced his red officer's cloak in half and gave half
to the beggar. That night in a dream he saw Christ, dressed in the
half-cloak and talking to the disciples. 'See,' he was saying, 'see
what a fine cloak Martin gave me today!'

Martin obtained a discharge from the army and was baptized.
In 360 he joined Bishop Hilary at Poitiers and founded a
monastery at Liguge, the first in Gaul. Martin was much influenced by the lives of the desert saints such as Antony and Paul
the Hermit, and longed for the opportunity to live in isolation
himself. But he was a charismatic figure and a born leader and
the Church, recognizing his gifts, appointed him Bishop of Tours
in 372. As an ex-soldier used to obeying orders, Martin submit-
ted to the will of the Church, but his teaching about living a
simple life and finding a desert place in a world of increasing
wealth and secularization came as a breath of fresh air. Young
men and women were drawn to his dynamic preaching.
Influenced by the lives of the desert Fathers, inspired by the
Gospel of St John and steeped in their love of the Psalms, these
young Christians left Tours each in search of their own 'desert'
place. Martin had launched the beginnings of a spiritual revolu-
tion.

Gospel
Matthew 25:31–46

Psalm
146

Collect
Eternal Lord God, Father of all mankind, through your servant Martin you have shown your love in the world. Grant us the same generosity of spirit that, loving you above all things, we may love also our fellow men and discern in each of them the spirit of your Son, our Saviour Jesus Christ.
    Amen.

17 November   *St Hilda of Whitby*

Sentence
The Lord will keep your going out and your coming in from this time forth and for evermore.   (Psalm 121:8 RSV)

Life
St Hilda was born in AD 614, into the Saxon royal families of Northumberland and East Anglia. In 627, along with her great-uncle Edwin, King of Northumbria, Hilda heard St Paulinus preach. She was just fourteen years of age and was so impressed that she was baptized by Paulinus that Easter in York. For nearly twenty years after that Hilda lived the life of a noblewoman at the royal palace of Yeavering.
    When Aidan came to Northumbria to preach, Hilda decided to become a nun. She started out to join her sister Hereswid at the convent in Chelles near Paris, but she had not travelled far when a message came from Aidan asking her to return. Aidan took her on as a student and gave her a small plot of land by the River Wear where she could make a hermitage. In 649 he made her abbess of a religious house at Hartlepool, which she ran in accordance with the rule of the Celtic Church. In 659 she founded a monastery for both men and women at Whitby.

Whitby became a centre for learning, where literature and the arts were encouraged and vocations fostered. The lay brother Caedmon, who stuttered badly, was encouraged to sing there, and the songs and stories he wrote helped those who could not read to understand the Scriptures.

Hilda and Cuthbert both worked tirelessly for a peaceful solution to the struggle between the Celtic and Roman Churches, and in 664 Hilda offered her monastery at Whitby as a meeting place for all the leaders. She hoped for reconciliation and perhaps compromise on both sides, and sided with St Colman in his arguments for the Celtic cause. But the brilliant Abbot Wilfred from Ripon spoke so eloquently on behalf of the Roman Church that the Synod decided that the Celtic Church must agree to come into line with Rome.

The Celtic delegates were bitterly disappointed. This, it seemed to them, was the end of the Celtic Church and the traditions they loved so much. Hilda, however, accepted defeat gracefully and loyally brought the monasteries under her control into line with Rome. Ten years later Hilda became unwell and remained ill for a further six years until she died in 680. On the night of her death, a nun at the monastery founded by Hilda in Hackness had a vision in which she saw Hilda's soul being borne up to heaven by a host of angels.

Gospel
Mark 14:3–9

Psalm
121

Collect
Eternal God and Father of us all, your servant Hilda gave her life into your service and brought about reconciliation and peace. Grant that in our lives we too may become peacemakers, so that

the sweet fragrance of our efforts may ascend to your kingdom
and give you joy.

Amen.

12 December   *St Corentin*

Sentence

For this God is our God for ever and ever : he shall be our guide
unto death.   (Psalm 48:13 BCP)

Life

St Corentin was a hermit who lived in Plomodiern in Brittany.
His hermitage overlooked the beautiful bay of Douarnez and
near his oratory was a small fountain that fell in a cascade to the sea.

In the stream running from the fountain there lived a miraculous fish, and according to legend Corentin cut a small piece
from it each day to serve as his daily meal, and the instant he put
the fish back in the water it became whole once more.

His reputation grew as a worker of miracles. He is recorded as
providing food and springs of water for strangers in need and for
many acts of healing. It was not long before the people of
Conauaille demanded that Corentin should be their first bishop.
According to tradition he was consecrated by St Martin himself,
but this cannot have been possible as well over a hundred years
separated the two saints. Such was the veneration of the people
for their bishop, however, that they naturally wanted to confer
on him the greatest of honours.

The seat of Corentin's see was in Quimper. Miracles continued to occur and money poured in to build and extend the
cathedral, the monasteries and the parishes that belonged to it.

Corentin proved to be a diligent and caring bishop. He was an
inspired preacher and converted many to the faith. Even after his
death, many miracles made his name a household word in
Brittany.

Gospel
Matthew 14:13–21

Psalm
48

Collect
Eternal God and Lord of all, you gave to your servant Corentin a great measure of faith. Through faith he was able to do many wondrous works. Through faith he gathered his flock around him and led them into your kingdom. Grant us, we beg you, a small measure of this faith, that in all humility we may strive to do your work in the world, and serve you with love and loyalty all the days of our lives.
    Amen.

For any Celtic saint

Sentence
The Lord is my light and my salvation; whom shall I fear? The Lord is the stronghold of my life; of whom shall I be afraid?

(Psalm 27:1 RSV)

Gospel
Matthew 5:13–16; Matthew 28:16–20; Mark 8:34–8; Mark 10:42–5; Luke 9:1–6; Luke 10:1–9; Luke 12:35–44; Luke 18:18–30; John 3:16–21

Psalm
15, 19, 27, 41, 84, 111, 115

Collect
Almighty Eternal God, by whose grace your servant .... left home and family to take the light of the gospel to unknown

lands, grant that we, in the same spirit of love, may give our lives in selfless devotion to you, so that through us your kingdom may come on earth and your will be done.

Amen.

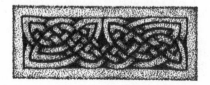

SELECTED PSALMS

Psalm 1

Blessed is the man that hath not walked in the counsel of the ungodly, nor stood in the way of sinners : and hath not sat in the seat of the scornful.

2 But his delight is in the law of the Lord : and in his law will he exercise himself day and night.

3 And he shall be like a tree planted by the water-side : that will bring forth his fruit in due season.

4 His leaf also shall not wither : and look, whatsoever he doeth, it shall prosper.

5 As for the ungodly, it is not so with them : but they are like the chaff, which the wind scattereth away from the face of the earth.

6 Therefore the ungodly shall not be able to stand in the judgement : neither the sinners in the congregation of the righteous.

7 But the Lord knoweth the way of the righteous : and the way of the ungodly shall perish.

Psalm 8

O Lord our Governor, how excellent is thy Name in all the world : thou that hast set thy glory above the heavens!

2 Out of the mouth of very babes and sucklings hast thou ordained strength, because of thine enemies : that thou mightest still the enemy and the avenger.

3 For I will consider thy heavens, even the works of thy fingers : the moon and the stars, which thou hast ordained.

4 What is man, that thou art mindful of him : and the son of man, that thou visitest him?

5 Thou madest him lower than the angels : to crown him with glory and worship.

6 Thou makest him to have dominion of the works of thy hands : and thou hast put all things in subjection under his feet;

7 All sheep and oxen : yea, and the beasts of the field;

8 The fowls of the air, and the fishes of the sea : and whatsoever walketh through the paths of the seas.

9 O Lord our Governor : how excellent is thy Name in all the world!

Psalm 15

Lord, who shall dwell in thy tabernacle : or who shall rest upon thy holy hill?

2 Even he that leadeth an uncorrupt life : and doeth the thing which is right, and speaketh the truth from his heart.

3 He that hath used no deceit in his tongue, nor done evil to his neighbour : and hath not slandered his neighbour.

4 He that setteth not by himself, but is lowly in his own eyes : and maketh much of them that fear the Lord.

5 He that sweareth unto his neighbour, and disappointeth him not : though it were to his own hindrance.

6 He that hath not given his money upon usury : nor taken reward against the innocent.

7 Whoso doeth these things : shall never fall.

Psalm 19

The heavens declare the glory of God : and the firmament sheweth his handy-work.

2 One day telleth another : and one night certifieth another.

3 There is neither speech nor language : but their voices are heard among them.

4 Their sound is gone out into all lands : and their words into the ends of the world.

5 In them hath he set a tabernacle for the sun : which cometh forth as a bridegroom out of his chamber, and rejoiceth as a giant to run his course.

6 It goeth forth from the uttermost part of the heaven, and runneth about unto the end of it again : and there is nothing hid from the heat thereof.

7 The law of the Lord is an undefiled law, converting the soul : the testimony of the Lord is sure, and giveth wisdom unto the simple.

8 The statutes of the Lord are right, and rejoice the heart : the commandment of the Lord is pure, and giveth light unto the eyes.

9 The fear of the Lord is clean, and endureth for ever : the judgements of the Lord are true, and righteous altogether.

10 More to be desired are they than gold, yea, than much fine gold : sweeter also than honey, and the honey-comb.

11 Moreover, by them is thy servant taught : and in keeping of them there is great reward.

12 Who can tell how oft he offendeth : O cleanse thou me from my secret faults.

13 Keep thy servant also from presumptuous sins, lest they get the dominion over me : so shall I be undefiled, and innocent from the great offence.

14 Let the words of my mouth, and the meditation of my heart : be alway acceptable in thy sight,

15 O Lord : my strength, and my redeemer.

Psalm 23

The Lord is my shepherd : therefore can I lack nothing.

2 He shall feed me in a green pasture : and lead me forth beside the waters of comfort.

3 He shall convert my soul : and bring me forth in the paths of righteousness, for his Name's sake.

4 Yea, though I walk through the valley of the shadow of death, I will fear no evil : for thou art with me; thy rod and thy staff comfort me.

5 Thou shalt prepare a table before me against them that trouble me : thou hast anointed my head with oil, and my cup shall be full.

6 But thy loving-kindness and mercy shall follow me all the days of my life : and I will dwell in the house of the Lord for ever.

Psalm 24

The earth is the Lord's, and all that therein is : the compass of the world, and they that dwell therein.

2 For he hath founded it upon the seas : and prepared it upon the floods.

3 Who shall ascend into the hill of the Lord : or who shall rise up in his holy place?

4 Even he that hath clean hands, and a pure heart : and that hath not lift up his mind unto vanity, nor sworn to deceive his neighbour.

5 He shall receive the blessing from the Lord : and righteousness from the God of his salvation.

6 This is the generation of them that seek him : even of them that seek thy face, O Jacob.

7 Lift up your heads, O ye gates, and be ye lift up, ye everlasting doors : and the King of glory shall come in.

8 Who is the King of glory : it is the Lord strong and mighty, even the Lord mighty in battle.

9 Lift up your heads, O ye gates, and be ye lift up, ye everlasting doors : and the King of glory shall come in.

10 Who is the King of glory : even the Lord of hosts, he is the King of glory.

Psalm 27

The Lord is my light and my salvation; whom then shall I fear : the Lord is the strength of my life; of whom then shall I be afraid?

2 When the wicked, even mine enemies and my foes, came upon me to eat up my flesh : they stumbled and fell.

3 Though an host of men were laid against me, yet shall not my heart be afraid : and though there rose up war against me, yet will I put my trust in him.

4 One thing have I desired of the Lord, which I will require : even that I may dwell in the house of the Lord all the days of my life, to behold the fair beauty of the Lord, and to visit his temple.

5 For in the time of trouble he shall hide me in his tabernacle : yea, in the secret place of his dwelling shall he hide me, and set me up upon a rock of stone.

6 And now shall he lift up mine head : above mine enemies round about me.

7 Therefore will I offer in his dwelling an oblation with great gladness : I will sing, and speak praises unto the Lord.

Psalm 29

Bring unto the Lord, O ye mighty, bring young rams unto the Lord : ascribe unto the Lord worship and strength.

2 Give the Lord the honour due unto his Name : worship the Lord with holy worship.

3 It is the Lord that commandeth the waters : it is the glorious God that maketh the thunder.

4 It is the Lord that ruleth the sea; the voice of the Lord is mighty in operation : the voice of the Lord is a glorious voice.

5 The voice of the Lord breaketh the cedar-trees : yea, the Lord breaketh the cedars of Libanus.

6 He maketh them also to skip like a calf : Libanus also, and Sirion, like a young unicorn.

7 The voice of the Lord divideth the flames of fire; the voice of the Lord shaketh the wilderness : yea, the Lord shaketh the wilderness of Cades.

8 The voice of the Lord maketh the hinds to bring forth young, and discovereth the thick bushes : in his temple doth every man speak of his honour.

9 The Lord sitteth above the water-flood : and the Lord remaineth a King for ever.

10 The Lord shall give strength unto his people : the Lord shall give his people the blessing of peace.

Psalm 42

Like as the hart desireth the water-brooks : so longeth my soul after thee, O God.

2 My soul is athirst for God, yea, even for the living God : when shall I come to appear before the presence of God?

3 My tears have been my meat day and night : while they daily say unto me, Where is now thy God?

4 Now when I think thereupon, I pour out my heart by myself : for I went with the multitude, and brought them forth into the house of God;

5 In the voice of praise and thanksgiving : among such as keep holy-day.

6 Why art thou so full of heaviness, O my soul : and why art thou so disquieted within me?

7 Put thy trust in God : for I will yet give him thanks for the help of his countenance.

8 My God, my soul is vexed within me : therefore will I remember thee concerning the land of Jordan, and the little hill of Hermon.

9 One deep calleth another, because of the noise of the waterpipes : all thy waves and storms are gone over me.

10 The Lord hath granted his loving-kindness in the day-time : and in the night-season did I sing of him, and made my prayer unto the God of my life.

11 I will say unto the God of my strength, Why hast thou forgotten me : why go I thus heavily, while the enemy oppresseth me?

12 My bones are smitten asunder as with a sword : while mine enemies that trouble me cast me in the teeth;

13 Namely, while they say daily unto me : Where is now thy God?

14 Why art thou so vexed, O my soul : and why art thou so disquieted within me?

15 O put thy trust in God : for I will yet thank him, which is the help of my countenance, and my God.

Psalm 46

God is our hope and strength : a very present help in trouble.

2 Therefore will we not fear, though the earth be moved : and though the hills be carried into the midst of the sea;

3 Though the waters thereof rage and swell : and though the mountains shake at the tempest of the same.

4 The rivers of the flood thereof shall make glad the city of God : the holy place of the tabernacle of the most Highest.

5 God is in the midst of her, therefore shall she not be removed : God shall help her, and that right early.

6 The heathen make much ado, and the kingdoms are moved :

but God hath shewed his voice, and the earth shall melt away.

7 The Lord of hosts is with us : the God of Jacob is our refuge.

8 O come hither, and behold the works of the Lord : what destruction he hath brought upon the earth.

9 He maketh wars to cease in all the world : he breaketh the bow, and knappeth the spear in sunder, and burneth the chariots in the fire.

10 Be still then, and know that I am God : I will be exalted among the heathen, and I will be exalted in the earth.

11 The Lord of hosts is with us : the God of Jacob is our refuge.

Psalm 48

Great is the Lord, and highly to be praised : in the city of our God, even upon his holy hill.

2 The hill of Sion is a fair place, and the joy of the whole earth : upon the north-side lieth the city of the great King; God is well known in her palaces as a sure refuge.

3 For lo, the kings of the earth : are gathered, and gone by together.

4 They marvelled to see such things : they were astonished, and suddenly cast down.

5 Fear came there upon them, and sorrow : as upon a woman in her travail.

6 Thou shalt break the ships of the sea : through the east-wind.

7 Like as we have heard, so have we seen in the city of the Lord of hosts, in the city of our God : God upholdeth the same for ever.

8 We wait for thy loving-kindness, O God : in the midst of thy temple.

9 O God, according to thy Name, so is thy praise unto the world's end : thy right hand is full of righteousness.

10 Let the mount Sion rejoice, and the daughter of Judah be glad : because of thy judgements.

11 Walk about Sion, and go round about her : and tell the towers thereof.

12 Mark well her bulwarks, set up her houses : that ye may tell them that come after.

13 For this God is our God for ever and ever : he shall be our guide unto death.

Psalm 63

O God, thou art my God : early will I seek thee.

2 My soul thirsteth for thee, my flesh also longeth after thee : in a barren and dry land where no water is.

3 Thus have I looked for thee in holiness : that I might behold thy power and glory.

4 For thy loving-kindness is better than the life itself : my lips shall praise thee.

5 As long as I live will I magnify thee on this manner : and lift up my hands in thy Name.

6 My soul shall be satisfied, even as it were with marrow and fatness : when my mouth praiseth thee with joyful lips.

7 Have I not remembered thee in my bed : and thought upon thee when I was waking?

8 Because thou hast been my helper : therefore under the shadow of thy wings will I rejoice.

9 My soul hangeth upon thee : thy right hand hath upholden me.

10 These also that seek the hurt of my soul : they shall go under the earth.

11 Let them fall upon the edge of the sword : that they may be a portion for foxes.

12 But the King shall rejoice in God; all they also that swear by him shall be commended : for the mouth of them that speak lies shall be stopped.

Psalm 77

I will cry unto God with my voice : even unto God will I cry with
my voice, and he shall hearken unto me.
2 In the time of my trouble I sought the Lord : my sore ran and
ceased not in the night-season; my soul refused comfort.
3 When I am in heaviness, I will think upon God : when my
heart is vexed, I will complain.
4 Thou holdest mine eyes waking : I am so feeble, that I cannot
speak.
5 I have considered the days of old : and the years that are past.
6 I call to remembrance my song : and in the night I commune
with mine own heart, and search out my spirits.
7 Will the Lord absent himself for ever : and will he be no more
intreated?
8 Is his mercy clean gone for ever : and is his promise come
utterly to an end for evermore?
9 Hath God forgotten to be gracious : and will he shut up his
loving-kindness in displeasure?
10 And I said, It is mine own infirmity : but I will remember the
years of the right hand of the most Highest.
11 I will remember the works of the Lord : and call to mind thy
wonders of old time.
12 I will think also of all thy works : and my talking shall be of
thy doings.
13 Thy way, O God, is holy : who is so great a God as our God?
14 Thou art the God that doeth wonders : and hast declared thy
power among the people.
15 Thou hast mightily delivered thy people : even the sons of
Jacob and Joseph.
16 The waters saw thee, O God, the waters saw thee, and were
afraid : the depths also were troubled.
17 The clouds poured out water, the air thundered : and thine
arrows went abroad.

18 The voice of thy thunder was heard round about : the lightnings shone upon the ground; the earth was moved, and shook withal.

19 Thy way is in the sea, and thy paths in the great waters : and thy footsteps are not known.

20 Thou leddest thy people like sheep : by the hand of Moses and Aaron.

Psalm 84

O how amiable are thy dwellings : thou Lord of hosts!

2 My soul hath a desire and longing to enter into the courts of the Lord : my heart and my flesh rejoice in the living God.

3 Yea, the sparrow hath found her an house, and the swallow a nest where she may lay her young : even thy altars, O Lord of hosts, my King and my God.

4 Blessed are they that dwell in thy house : they will be alway praising thee.

5 Blessed is the man whose strength is in thee : in whose heart are thy ways.

6 Who going through the vale of misery use it for a well : and the pools are filled with water.

7 They will go from strength to strength : and unto the God of gods appeareth every one of them in Sion.

8 O Lord God of hosts, hear my prayer : hearken, O God of Jacob.

9 Behold, O God our defender : and look upon the face of thine Anointed.

10 For one day in thy courts : is better than a thousand.

11 I had rather be a door-keeper in the house of my God : than to dwell in the tents of ungodliness.

12 For the Lord God is a light and defence : the Lord will give grace and worship, and no good thing shall he withhold from them that live a godly life.

13 O Lord God of hosts : blessed is the man that putteth his trust in thee.

Psalm 91

Whoso dwelleth under the defence of the most High : shall abide under the shadow of the Almighty.

2 I will say unto the Lord, Thou art my hope, and my strong hold : my God, in him will I trust.

3 For he shall deliver thee from the snare of the hunter : and from the noisome pestilence.

4 He shall defend thee under his wings, and thou shalt be safe under his feathers : his faithfulness and truth shall be thy shield and buckler.

5 Thou shalt not be afraid for any terror by night : nor for the arrow that flieth by day;

6 For the pestilence that walketh in darkness : nor for the sickness that destroyeth in the noon-day.

7 A thousand shall fall beside thee, and ten thousand at thy right hand : but it shall not come nigh thee.

8 Yea, with thine eyes shalt thou behold : and see the reward of the ungodly.

9 For thou, Lord, art my hope : thou hast set thine house of defence very high.

10 There shall no evil happen unto thee : neither shall any plague come nigh thy dwelling.

11 For he shall give his angels charge over thee : to keep thee in all thy ways.

12 They shall bear thee in their hands : that thou hurt not thy foot against a stone.

13 Thou shalt go upon the lion and adder : the young lion and the dragon shalt thou tread under thy feet.

14 Because he hath set his love upon me, therefore will I deliver him : I will set him up, because he hath known my Name.

15 He shall call upon me, and I will hear him : yea, I am with him in trouble; I will deliver him, and bring him to honour.
16 With long life will I satisfy him : and shew him my salvation.

Psalm 93

The Lord is King, and hath put on glorious apparel : the Lord hath put on his apparel, and girded himself with strength.
2 He hath made the round world so sure : that it cannot be moved.
3 Ever since the world began hath thy seat been prepared : thou art from everlasting.
4 The floods are risen, O Lord, the floods have lift up their voice : the floods lift up their waves.
5 The waves of the sea are mighty, and rage horribly : but yet the Lord, who dwelleth on high, is mightier.
6 Thy testimonies, O Lord, are very sure : holiness becometh thine house for ever.

Psalm 96

O sing unto the Lord a new song : sing unto the Lord, all the whole earth.
2 Sing unto the Lord, and praise his Name : be telling of his salvation from day to day.
3 Declare his honour unto the heathen : and his wonders unto all people.
4 For the Lord is great, and cannot worthily be praised : he is more to be feared than all gods.
5 As for all the gods of the heathen, they are but idols : but it is the Lord that made the heavens.
6 Glory and worship are before him : power and honour are in his sanctuary.

7 Ascribe unto the Lord, O ye kindreds of the people : ascribe unto the Lord worship and power.

8 Ascribe unto the Lord the honour due unto his Name : bring presents, and come into his courts.

9 O worship the Lord in the beauty of holiness : let the whole earth stand in awe of him.

10 Tell it out among the heathen that the Lord is King : and that it is he who hath made the round world so fast that it cannot be moved; and how that he shall judge the people righteously.

11 Let the heavens rejoice, and let the earth be glad : let the sea make a noise, and all that therein is.

12 Let the field be joyful, and all that is in it : then shall all the trees of the wood rejoice before the Lord.

13 For he cometh, for he cometh to judge the earth : and with righteousness to judge the world, and the people with his truth.

Psalm 98

O sing unto the Lord a new song : for he hath done marvellous things.

2 With his own right hand, and with his holy arm : hath he gotten himself the victory.

3 The Lord declared his salvation : his righteousness hath he openly shewed in the sight of the heathen.

4 He hath remembered his mercy and truth toward the house of Israel : and all the ends of the world have seen the salvation of our God.

5 Shew yourselves joyful unto the Lord, all ye lands : sing, rejoice, and give thanks.

6 Praise the Lord upon the harp : sing to the harp with a psalm of thanksgiving.

7 With trumpets also and shawms : O shew yourselves joyful before the Lord the King.

8 Let the sea make a noise, and all that therein is : the round world, and they that dwell therein.

9 Let the floods clap their hands, and let the hills be joyful together before the Lord : for he is come to judge the earth.

10 With righteousness shall he judge the world : and the people with equity.

Psalm 99

The Lord is King, be the people never so unpatient : he sitteth between the cherubims, be the earth never so unquiet.

2 The Lord is great in Sion : and high above all people.

3 They shall give thanks unto thy Name : which is great, wonderful, and holy.

4 The King's power loveth judgement; thou hast prepared equity : thou hast executed judgement and righteousness in Jacob.

5 O magnify the Lord our God : and fall down before his footstool, for he is holy.

6 Moses and Aaron among his priests, and Samuel among such as call upon his Name : these called upon the Lord, and he heard them.

7 He spake unto them out of the cloudy pillar : for they kept his testimonies, and the law that he gave them.

8 Thou heardest them, O Lord our God : thou forgavest them, O God, and punishedst their own inventions.

9 O magnify the Lord our God, and worship him upon his holy hill : for the Lord our God is holy.

Psalm 100

O be joyful in the Lord, all ye lands : serve the Lord with gladness, and come before his presence with a song.

2 Be ye sure that the Lord he is God : it is he that hath made us, and not we ourselves; we are his people, and the sheep of his pasture.

3 O go your way into his gates with thanksgiving, and into his courts with praise : be thankful unto him, and speak good of his Name.

4 For the Lord is gracious, his mercy is everlasting : and his truth endureth from generation to generation.

Psalm 103

Praise the Lord, O my soul : and all that is within me praise his holy Name.

2 Praise the Lord, O my soul : and forget not all his benefits;

3 Who forgiveth all thy sin : and healeth all thine infirmities;

4 Who saveth thy life from destruction : and crowneth thee with mercy and loving-kindness;

5 Who satisfieth thy mouth with good things : making thee young and lusty as an eagle.

6 The Lord executeth righteousness and judgement : for all them that are oppressed with wrong.

7 He shewed his ways unto Moses : his works unto the children of Israel.

8 The Lord is full of compassion and mercy : long-suffering, and of great goodness.

9 He will not alway be chiding : neither keepeth he his anger for ever.

10 He hath not dealt with us after our sins : nor rewarded us according to our wickednesses.

11 For look how high the heaven is in comparison of the earth : so great is his mercy also toward them that fear him.

12 Look how wide also the east is from the west : so far hath he set our sins from us.

13 Yea, like as a father pitieth his own children : even so is the Lord merciful unto them that fear him.

14 For he knoweth whereof we are made : he remembereth that we are but dust.

15 The days of man are but as grass : for he flourisheth as a flower of the field.

16 For as soon as the wind goeth over it, it is gone : and the place thereof shall know it no more.

17 But the merciful goodness of the Lord endureth for ever and ever upon them that fear him : and his righteousness upon children's children;

18 Even upon such as keep his covenant : and think upon his commandments to do them.

19 The Lord hath prepared his seat in heaven : and his kingdom ruleth over all.

20 O praise the Lord, ye angels of his, ye that excel in strength : ye that fulfil his commandment, and hearken unto the voice of his words.

21 O praise the Lord, all ye his hosts : ye servants of his that do his pleasure.

22 O speak good of the Lord, all ye works of his, in all places of his dominion : praise thou the Lord, O my soul.

Psalm 111

I will give thanks unto the Lord with my whole heart : secretly among the faithful, and in the congregation.

2 The works of the Lord are great : sought out of all them that have pleasure therein.

3 His work is worthy to be praised and had in honour : and his righteousness endureth for ever.

4 The merciful and gracious Lord hath so done his marvellous works : that they ought to be had in remembrance.

5 He hath given meat unto them that fear him : he shall ever be mindful of his covenant.

6 He hath shewed his people the power of his works : that he may give them the heritage of the heathen.

7 The works of his hands are verity and judgement : all his commandments are true.

8 They stand fast for ever and ever : and are done in truth and equity.

9 He sent redemption unto his people : he hath commanded his covenant for ever; holy and reverend is his Name.

10 The fear of the Lord is the beginning of wisdom : a good understanding have all they that do thereafter; the praise of it endureth for ever.

Psalm 119

Teach me, O Lord, the way of thy statutes : and I shall keep it unto the end.

34 Give me understanding, and I shall keep thy law : yea, I shall keep it with my whole heart.

35 Make me to go in the path of thy commandments : for therein is my desire.

36 Incline my heart unto thy testimonies : and not to covetousness.

37 O turn away mine eyes, lest they behold vanity : and quicken thou me in thy way.

38 O stablish thy word in thy servant : that I may fear thee.

39 Take away the rebuke that I am afraid of : for thy judgements are good.

40 Behold, my delight is in thy commandments : O quicken me in thy righteousness.

41 Let thy loving mercy come also unto me, O Lord : even thy salvation, according unto thy word.

42 So shall I make answer unto my blasphemers : for my trust is in thy word.

43 O take not the word of thy truth utterly out of my mouth : for my hope is in thy judgements.

44 So shall I alway keep thy law : yea, for ever and ever.

45 And I will walk at liberty : for I seek thy commandments.

46 I will speak of thy testimonies also, even before kings : and will not be ashamed.

47 And my delight shall be in thy commandments : which I have loved.

48 My hands also will I lift up unto thy commandments, which I have loved : and my study shall be in thy statutes.

Psalm 121

I will lift up mine eyes unto the hills : from whence cometh my help.

2 My help cometh even from the Lord : who hath made heaven and earth.

3 He will not suffer thy foot to be moved : and he that keepeth thee will not sleep.

4 Behold, he that keepeth Israel : shall neither slumber nor sleep.

5 The Lord himself is thy keeper : the Lord is thy defence upon thy right hand;

6 So that the sun shall not burn thee by day : neither the moon by night.

7 The Lord shall preserve thee from all evil : yea, it is even he that shall keep thy soul.

8 The Lord shall preserve thy going out, and thy coming in : from this time forth for evermore.

Psalm 122

I was glad when they said unto me : We will go into the house of the Lord.

2 Our feet shall stand in thy gates : O Jerusalem.

3 Jerusalem is built as a city : that is at unity in itself.

4 For thither the tribes go up, even the tribes of the Lord : to testify unto Israel, to give thanks unto the Name of the Lord.

5 For there is the seat of judgement : even the seat of the house of David.

6 O pray for the peace of Jerusalem : they shall prosper that love thee.

7 Peace be within thy walls : and plenteousness within thy palaces.

8 For my brethren and companions' sakes : I will wish thee prosperity.

9 Yea, because of the house of the Lord our God : I will seek to do thee good.

Psalm 133

Behold, how good and joyful a thing it is : brethren, to dwell together in unity!

2 It is like the precious ointment upon the head, that ran down unto the beard : even unto Aaron's beard, and went down to the skirts of his clothing.

3 Like as the dew of Hermon : which fell upon the hill of Sion.

4 For there the Lord promised his blessing : and life for evermore.

Psalm 138

I will give thanks unto thee, O Lord, with my whole heart : even before the gods will I sing praise unto thee.

2 I will worship toward thy holy temple, and praise thy Name, because of thy loving-kindness and truth : for thou hast magnified thy Name and thy word above all things.

3 When I called upon thee, thou heardest me : and enduedst my soul with much strength.

4 All the kings of the earth shall praise thee, O Lord : for they have heard the words of thy mouth.

5 Yea, they shall sing in the ways of the Lord : that great is the glory of the Lord.

6 For though the Lord be high, yet hath he respect unto the lowly : as for the proud, he beholdeth them afar off.

7 Though I walk in the midst of trouble, yet shalt thou refresh me : thou shalt stretch forth thy hand upon the furiousness of mine enemies, and thy right hand shall save me.

8 The Lord shall make good his loving-kindness toward me : yea, thy mercy, O Lord, endureth for ever; despise not then the works of thine own hands.

Psalm 139

O Lord, thou hast searched me out and known me : thou knowest my down-sitting and mine up-rising, thou understandest my thoughts long before.

2 Thou art about my path, and about my bed : and spiest out all my ways.

3 For lo, there is not a word in my tongue : but thou, O Lord, knowest it altogether.

4 Thou hast fashioned me behind and before : and laid thine hand upon me.

5 Such knowledge is too wonderful and excellent for me : I cannot attain unto it.

6 Whither shall I go then from thy Spirit : or whither shall I go then from thy presence?

7 If I climb up into heaven, thou art there : if I go down to hell, thou art there also.

8 If I take the wings of the morning : and remain in the uttermost parts of the sea;

9 Even there also shall thy hand lead me : and thy right hand shall hold me.

10 If I say, Peradventure the darkness shall cover me : then shall my night be turned to day.

11 Yea, the darkness is no darkness with thee, but the night is as clear as the day : the darkness and light to thee are both alike.

12 For my reins are thine : thou hast covered me in my mother's womb.

13 I will give thanks unto thee, for I am fearfully and wonderfully made : marvellous are thy works, and that my soul knoweth right well.

Psalm 146

Praise the Lord, O my soul; while I live will I praise the Lord : yea, as long as I have any being, I will sing praises unto my God.

2 O put not your trust in princes, nor in any child of man : for there is no help in them.

3 For when the breath of man goeth forth he shall turn again to his earth : and then all his thoughts perish.

4 Blessed is he that hath the God of Jacob for his help : and whose hope is in the Lord his God;

5 Who made heaven and earth, the sea, and all that therein is : who keepeth his promise for ever;

6 Who helpeth them to right that suffer wrong : who feedeth the hungry.

7 The Lord looseth men out of prison : the Lord giveth sight to the blind.

8 The Lord helpeth them that are fallen : the Lord careth for the righteous.

9 The Lord careth for the strangers : he defendeth the fatherless and widow : as for the way of the ungodly, he turneth it upside down.

10 The Lord thy God, O Sion, shall be King for evermore : and throughout all generations.

Psalm 148

O praise the Lord of heaven : praise him in the height.

2 Praise him, all ye angels of his : praise him, all his host.

3 Praise him, sun and moon : praise him, all ye stars and light.

4 Praise him, all ye heavens : and ye waters that are above the heavens.

5 Let them praise the Name of the Lord : for he spake the word, and they were made; he commanded, and they were created.

6 He hath made them fast for ever and ever : he hath given them a law which shall not be broken.

7 Praise the Lord upon earth : ye dragons, and all deeps;

8 Fire and hail, snow and vapours : wind and storm, fulfilling his word;

9 Mountains and all hills : fruitful trees and all cedars;

10 Beasts and all cattle : worms and feathered fowls;

11 Kings of the earth and all people : princes and all judges of the world;

12 Young men and maidens, old men and children, praise the Name of the Lord : for his Name only is excellent, and his praise above heaven and earth.

13 He shall exalt the horn of his people; all his saints shall praise him : even the children of Israel, even the people that serveth him.

▨▨▨ hIStORIcAL OVERVIEW

Dateline

BC	2400	Beaker People
	700	Iron Age A
	400	Iron Age B

AD	43	Romans settle in Britain
	276	Antony in Egypt
	312	Emperor Constantine becomes Christian
	337	Martin
	340	Jerome
	360	Ninian
	380	Pelagius
	389	Patrick
	410	Romans leave Britain
		King Arthur, Kea, Brychan, Levan
	450	Illtyd
	490	Samson, Guenole, Paul, Ailbe
	520	Columba
	550	David, Petroc
	597	Augustine lands in Kent
	615	King Athelfrith massacres 1,200 monks in Bangor
	635	Aidan goes to Northumbria
	664	Cuthbert is made Prior in Lindisfarne
		Hilda and the Council of Whitby

Celtic pagan festivals

Samhain (New Year)   1 November – 31 January
Imbolc (Spring)   1 February – 30 April
Beltane (Summer)   1 May – 31 July
Lughnasa (Harvest)   1 August – 31 October

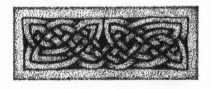